NATO
Enlargement
2000–2015

Determinants and Implications for Defense Planning and Shaping

Thomas S. Szayna

Project AIR FORCE

RAND

Prepared for the United States Air Force

The research reported here was sponsored by the United States Air Force under Contract F49642-96-C-0001. Further information may be obtained from the Strategic Planning Division, Directorate of Plans, Hq USAF.

Library of Congress Cataloging-in-Publication Data

Szayna, Thomas S., [DATE]
   NATO enlargement, 2000–2015 : determinants and implications for defense planning and shaping / Thomas S. Szayna.
      p. cm.
   Includes bibliographical references.
   "MR-1243."
   ISBN 0-8330-2961-4
   1. North Atlantic Treaty Organization—Membership. 2. Military planning—Europe. 3. United States—Military policy. 4. Air forces—Europe. I. Title.

UA646.3 .S977 2001
355'.031091821—dc21

                                                                    2001020492

RAND is a nonprofit institution that helps improve policy and decisionmaking through research and analysis. RAND® is a registered trademark. RAND's publications do not necessarily reflect the opinions or policies of its research sponsors.

Cover designed by Maritta Tapanainen

Published 2001 by RAND
1700 Main Street, P.O. Box 2138, Santa Monica, CA 90407-2138
1200 South Hayes Street, Arlington, VA 22202-5050
RAND URL: http://www.rand.org/
To order RAND documents or to obtain additional information, contact Distribution Services: Telephone: (310) 451-7002; Fax: (310) 451-6915; Internet: order@rand.org

In January 1994, NATO committed itself to a gradual process of enlargement, and in 1999, it admitted three new members—Poland, Hungary, and the Czech Republic. A further enlargement decision is scheduled for 2002, with a new member (or members) possibly joining NATO in 2004. Over the next 15 years, as many as three decisions could be made on further enlargement. These decisions and the overall course of enlargement will pose many far-reaching strategic and military challenges for NATO policymakers. Which countries are likely to be admitted, and when? What is the status of the armed forces of potential member countries? What impact will the accession of new members have on NATO's main missions?

This report develops and applies an analytical framework to evaluate potential members' relative readiness for and likelihood of admission to NATO. The framework takes into account political, strategic, and military criteria. The purpose of the analysis is to inform decisionmaking by the United States Air Force, the United States European Command (EUCOM), and EUCOM component commands regarding shaping actions (with a particular emphasis on airpower) toward the aspiring members.

The research presented here is part of a larger project on the changing strategic environment in and around Europe and its implications for the United States and NATO. Sponsored by the Commander, United States Air Forces in Europe, and the Deputy Chief of Staff for Air and Space Operations, Headquarters, United States Air Force, the project was conducted in the Strategy and Doctrine Program of RAND's Project AIR FORCE.

This report should be of interest to those engaged in policymaking regarding European security. Its specific military focus is on air forces, but its discussion of the defense planning implications of the enlargement process and the engagement and shaping recommendations is also relevant to other dimensions of military power.

For comments and further information, please contact the author: Tom_Szayna@rand.org

PROJECT AIR FORCE

Project AIR FORCE (PAF), a division of RAND, is the United States Air Force's federally funded research and development center (FFRDC) for studies and analyses. It provides the Air Force with independent analyses of policy alternatives affecting the development, employment, combat readiness, and support of current and future air and space forces. Research is carried out in four programs: Aerospace Force Development; Manpower, Personnel, and Training; Resource Management; and Strategy and Doctrine.

CONTENTS

FIGURES

TABLES

SUMMARY

Having committed itself to gradual enlargement in 1994, NATO took the important step of admitting Poland, Hungary, and the Czech Republic as members in 1999. But even though NATO's enlargement has received an enormous amount of public attention, NATO's transformation in the 1990s is probably the more important of the two steps NATO has taken. Created as an organization dedicated to the collective defense of its members, NATO transformed itself in the 1990s, expanding its mission to include conflict prevention and conflict management throughout Europe, including beyond the boundaries of the NATO treaty area. Both of these processes, enlargement and transformation, have been driven primarily by political imperatives—that is, not by a sense of direct threat, but by an environment-shaping agenda of democratization and integration.

NATO's transformation and its enlargement process have profound military implications for the United States and its allies. This report presents a framework for thinking about the determinants of future enlargement, the specific defense challenges they pose, and the shaping policies that might help to address some of the challenges.

CONTEXT

NATO's enlargement and transformation are taking place within a benign security environment that has prevailed in Europe since the late 1990s, an environment characterized by the absence (or extremely low incidence) of armed conflict and the lack of near-term potential for a major war. This environment has come about in no small part as a result of NATO's transformation into an organization focusing on conflict prevention and conflict management. NATO's self-designation as an institution for upholding peace and security throughout Europe means that some leaders in the "unintegrated" part of Europe (i.e., essentially the former communist states in Europe) who otherwise might be willing to use force to pursue their goals now have to modify their behavior to take NATO's potential re-action into account. Conversely, countries in this region that abide by a set of norms meant to advance democratic internal develop-ment and cooperative international behavior are offered the possi-bility of full NATO membership.

Put bluntly, NATO's current strategy resembles the proverbial carrot and stick. NATO's enlargement offers membership (the carrot) to encourage peaceful transformation and integration into a larger European security community, and NATO's transformation (into a conflict prevention and management organization) provides the co-ercive component (the stick) that can be used to enforce peace and deter aggression in and around Europe.

As part of the enlargement process, NATO has established pre-conditions for consideration of new members, almost all of which involve internal democratic reforms rather than military considera-tions. In addition, NATO has identified nine countries as being on track to membership through its Membership Action Plan (MAP). Participation in MAP and fulfillment of the pre-accession criteria do not guarantee that a country will become a member, however. As the 1997–99 round of enlargement showed, strategic considerations also play a role in determining which countries are invited to join and when.

One complication that arises from NATO's transformation and en-largement is that the line dividing its members and non-members has become blurred. Although this blurring is intentional and con-tributes to the continuation of a benign security environment, it creates difficulties for defense planning. By taking on a responsibil-ity for European security as a whole and identifying specific coun-tries as possible future members, NATO has extended implicit and conditional security guarantees to many non-member states, such as the MAP countries.

FRAMEWORK FOR THINKING ABOUT NATO'S FUTURE ENLARGEMENT

Although the line between membership in and close association with NATO has been blurred, the differences have not disappeared. Moreover, military planning needs to take into account whether a given state is likely to be a NATO member soon or will continue in its MAP status (with the associated implicit guarantee) for a considerable period of time. This report develops a methodology for military planners to use in discerning the likelihood of NATO membership for specific countries within the next 10 to 15 years. First, the ability of individual countries to meet NATO's pre-conditions for membership is assessed using military, political, and economic criteria. Then, a series of cost-benefit analyses is performed to assess a vaguer but probably more important element of the process—the strategic rationale for inviting particular countries into NATO. These two analyses produce an overall assessment of a country's likelihood of accession.

Findings

The methodology's use leads to the following conclusions regarding the dozen or so countries that could conceivably join NATO in the next 10 to 15 years:

- Of the MAP states, Slovenia is the most qualified and attractive candidate for membership from NATO's strategic perspective. The costs of Slovene integration will be virtually nil, and the benefits, though small, will be potentially significant in view of NATO's focus on the Balkans.

- Slovakia is next in line. Its slightly lower overall attractiveness compared with Slovenia is mitigated by its relatively larger and more modern armed forces. Slovakia straddles the northern and southern axis of NATO's enlargement; the costs of its integration will be low, and the benefits will be modest but visible.

- Estonia, Lithuania, and Latvia are mid-term (or longer) candidates. Their advanced stage in meeting NATO's criteria is offset by the strategic ramifications of their accession.

- Bulgaria and Romania follow. Their relative strategic attractiveness is offset by their inability to meet NATO's criteria.

- Macedonia and especially Albania are the least advanced in meeting NATO's criteria. Their prospects for membership are distinctly long-term, and current activities center on their evolving into real candidates.

- Of the EU members currently not in NATO, Austria is in a good position to join if it chooses to do so. To a lesser extent, so is Sweden. Finnish membership, however, would entail some difficulties because of the strategic costs it would impose on NATO.

The positions just described are in no way permanent, since the assessments assume a continuing evolution along the path currently being followed, and an individual country's course always can change. In particular, projections other than those for the two clear choices of Slovenia and Slovakia are subject to considerable uncertainty. Moreover, were the security environment to unexpectedly shift away from its current trends, the reasoning behind these assessments also might shift. The changed circumstances might mean, for example, that enlargement could proceed at a faster pace and with relaxed accession criteria.

MILITARY FORCES OF POTENTIAL MEMBERS

Given their limited manpower and generally low technological sophistication, training, and readiness levels, the individual MAP states have the potential to make only minor (though not irrelevant) military contributions to NATO in terms of collective defense and power projection over the next 10 to 15 years. For the foreseeable future, ground forces will continue to dominate these states' militaries, and defense budgets (except for that of Slovenia) will continue to be much smaller than those of current NATO members of similar size.

One of the most significant problems facing the MAP states is modernization of their air forces. Three of the armed forces (those of Slovakia, Romania, and Bulgaria) have experience with advanced (fourth-generation) combat aircraft and field small numbers of modern aircraft. The six others, however, are in the process of building their air forces and currently possess little equipment of any kind, which means they cannot now ensure their own air sovereignty and probably will not be able to in the near future and perhaps beyond. All of the MAP states' air forces face problems of low aircraft service-ability and limited availability of aircrew training. And because of their budgetary problems, even if the MAP states were to obtain NATO-compatible advanced jet aircraft, they most likely could not afford to operate them at levels approaching NATO standards. The MAP states could more meaningfully contribute to NATO air opera-tions through army aviation (e.g., transport and attack helicopters), which would be a natural complement to the MAP states' focus on ground forces. But probably the greatest contribution they could make is to allow NATO uninhibited access to their airspace and to provide quality infrastructure to support NATO's missions in and around Europe. Because of their NATO aspirations, the MAP states are likely to be receptive to NATO's requests for access to their airspace and infrastructure.

DIRECTIONS FOR SHAPING

A well thought-out plan of development and a wise investment of funds could allow each MAP state eventually to make a meaningful, if modest, military contribution to NATO. Because of the leverage it has as a result of the incentive structure it established for the MAP states, NATO is uniquely positioned to help ensure that force devel-opment in the MAP states proceeds with a large measure of effi-ciency.

To be appropriate, the shaping strategy used by the United States and its allies needs to incorporate an understanding of the following key issues:

- The extent of the potential strategic exposure and need for NATO reinforcement that accompany hypothetical threats to a MAP state under crisis conditions.

- The time frame for a MAP state likely joining NATO.

- The severity of the problems a MAP state faces with its armed forces (including the difference between "oversized" and "emerging" militaries, which also indicates how applicable the lessons learned from NATO's integration of Poland, the Czech Republic, and Hungary will be).

- The means available to a MAP state for addressing the problems of its armed forces.

- The likely useful (technologically sophisticated and well-trained) contribution of a MAP state to NATO's peace operations.

Specific recommendations for the development of their armed forces, particularly air forces, should flow from these distinctions.

As the accession of Poland, the Czech Republic, and Hungary shows, integration of the MAP militaries into NATO will be a long and difficult process. The problems are especially acute in the realm of air forces and air defense. But whatever priorities emerge and whatever their specific order, what is clearly needed is a long-term phased strategy of development and integration for potential members that would serve both to prepare these countries for eventual NATO membership and to enhance near-term deterrence. NATO has the leverage and the means of influence to help coordinate the MAP states' choices and to assist countries in working toward optimal use of their resources and capabilities.

ACKNOWLEDGMENTS

I am grateful to Ben Lambeth and Christopher Bowie for reviewing an earlier version of this document. Zalmay Khalilzad, David Ochmanek, Ian Lesser, William O'Malley, and Peter Ryan also took time to comment on earlier versions of this report. Among the many USAF officers and civilians, the following were especially helpful during the course of my research: Colonel David Larivee, Captain Mark Wills, Major David Whitt, Captain Dave Scanlon, Lieutenant Colonel Rod Zastrow, Brian Fishpaugh, and Mark Butler. Kristin Leuschner provided valuable comments on the report's structure and organization, and Jeri O'Donnell had the unenviable task of editing the document. Special thanks go to Roy Gates and Pamela Thompson for putting together the report's maps.

Chapter One

INTRODUCTION

Having committed itself to gradual enlargement in 1994, NATO took the important step of admitting Poland, Hungary, and the Czech Republic as members in 1999. But even though NATO's enlargement has received an enormous amount of public attention, NATO's transformation in the 1990s is probably the more important of the two steps NATO has taken. Created as an organization dedicated to the collective defense of its members, NATO has now expanded its mission to include conflict prevention and conflict management throughout Europe, including beyond the boundaries of the NATO treaty area. In both its enlargement and its transformation, NATO has been driven primarily by political imperatives—that is, not by a sense of direct threat, but by an environment-shaping agenda of democratization and integration.

The military implications of NATO's enlargement and transformation for the United States and its allies are profound. NATO's transformed role entails missions for which the armed forces of many of its current members remain underprepared, and the accession of each new member extends the NATO commitment to the collective defense of all members, even if there is currently no apparent threat to a new member. The commitment entails a multitude of military preparations to ensure that if a threat were to materialize, the commitment would not be hollow. Such preparations are necessary for deterrence, to help ensure that a threat does not materialize in the first place.

NATO's transformation and the way that NATO enlargement has unfolded have in some ways blurred the line dividing NATO members and non-members, making military planning more complex. By taking on a larger responsibility for European security as a whole and identifying specific countries as potential future members, NATO may be seen as having extended an implicit security guarantee to non-member states. At the same time, NATO membership entails a unique level of cooperation, trust, and specific preparations for joint operations, all of which become more complicated as NATO's size increases. For military planning purposes, the U.S. armed services and the United States European Command (EUCOM) must be able to accurately identify whether and, if so, when a particular country might join NATO. Nearly a dozen countries make up the "long list" of potential NATO members—i.e., those that could conceivably join within the next 10 to 15 years—and some of these candidates present significant challenges for defense planning, even in the benign security environment that currently exists in Europe. If the situation changes for the worse, the membership and/or the defense responsibilities for probable members could increase greatly.

Forecasting the likelihood of a given country's accession to NATO is a complex endeavor, particularly because of the political rationale driving the process. The United States will likely be the main decisionmaker in any future NATO enlargement, as it was during the initial round in 1997–99. The final decision, however, will be made within a NATO framework and will be subject to the political preferences of NATO's main members, as well as to intra-alliance bargaining.

STUDY OBJECTIVE AND SCOPE

This report is designed to assist the U.S. Air Force in preparing for NATO's continuing evolution and enlargement in the next decade and beyond. It offers a framework for gauging the likelihood that specific countries aspiring to NATO membership will become members, and it presents guidelines for arriving at the general time frame in which a given country might become a NATO member.[1] In addi-

---

[1]The guidelines are meant to be used by military planners to assist them in predicting political outcomes. The author is well aware of the pitfalls associated with predictions, and the forecasts should be taken as elaborations stemming from a current rundown of the criteria developed for assessing the likelihood of accession. Should the circum-

tion, the report provides an overview of the problems prospective members face in terms of their armed forces, especially their air forces, as well as shaping guidelines and priorities for U.S. planners regarding these armed forces.

REPORT ORGANIZATION AND APPROACH

The report consists of five chapters. Chapter Two establishes the context for thinking about contemporary defense planning in Europe, using as its starting point the overall benign security environment that currently exists in Europe and that stems, in no small part, from NATO's transforming itself into an organization whose mission includes aspects of collective and cooperative security. This chapter establishes the background for NATO's enlargement and defines NATO's criteria for new members.

Chapter Three examines the unfolding of the post–Cold War enlargement to date. It traces out an identifiable pattern in the process and provides parameters for how future enlargement is likely to evolve in relation to an informal five-step process to accession that NATO has put in place.

Chapters Four and Five constitute the core of the analysis. Chapter Four provides a framework for thinking about the likelihood of specific countries joining NATO in the foreseeable future and presents an analytical tool for assessing the readiness and attractiveness of aspiring members. The analysis focuses chiefly on the nine countries on track to membership through the Membership Action Plan (MAP), each of which is evaluated using both the explicit pre-conditions established by NATO and the unstated but dominant strategic criteria that govern NATO decisions. Two scales are devised for assessing the MAP countries—one for along the explicit criteria, and one for along the implicit criteria—and a final assessment is made by combining the two.

Chapter Five presents the military implications of the enlargement process, assessing the armed forces of the MAP states. The major challenges facing all the MAP states are analyzed, as are the special

stances concerning some of the criteria change, as they almost certainly will, a reevaluation (using the framework provided here) will be in order.

problems of particular countries. Like the three countries that joined NATO in 1999, the MAP states face particular challenges with regard to their air force capabilities.

Chapter Six reviews the major problems facing the MAP countries and discusses the complications NATO faces as a result of these countries being placed on the membership track. A list of recommendations to guide the USAF and EUCOM in their planning processes is provided, along with specific actions that planners might consider for shaping the situation to U.S. and NATO advantage, particularly for support of U.S. goals in Europe.

The data used to inform this report were drawn from primary documents (NATO materials) and secondary literature, supplemented by interviews with former U.S. officials to NATO and defense representatives of countries aspiring to NATO membership. The report is based on information available as of the end of 2000.

Chapter Two

THE PLANNING CONTEXT

NATO's transformation to an organization whose mission places greater emphasis on collective and cooperative security has important implications for its enlargement process. These implications are the subject of this chapter. Central to this discussion are the issues inherent to NATO's enlargement strategy, issues that will likely come to the fore as NATO makes its next enlargement decision. From the perspective of the United States and its allies, perhaps the most significant question is how further NATO enlargement could affect NATO's ability to provide for the collective defense in the context of gray-area commitments to non-NATO countries. Included in this chapter is an examination of the various levels of NATO commitments and a discussion of their potential military implications.

CONTEMPORARY EUROPEAN SECURITY ENVIRONMENT

NATO's current strategy for enlargement is both the result of and a contributor to the benign security environment that currently prevails in Europe. This environment is characterized by the absence (or extremely low incidence) of armed conflict and the lack of any near-term potential for a major war. From the standpoint of U.S. interest in peaceful and democratic development in Europe, the current European security environment, when compared with the situation in the 1980s or early 1990s, represents a remarkably positive turn of events.

If incidence of armed conflict is used as a measure,[1] Europe is the most peaceful continent in the world. Since 1996, Europe has had the fewest armed conflicts of the world's five continents/regions.[2] The early part of the 1990s witnessed a brief upsurge in the incidence of armed conflict on the European continent. But after reaching a high point in 1993, the upsurge, caused mainly by the fall of communism and the sometimes violent dissolution of the communist federal states, declined. Following NATO's involvement in ending the strife in former Yugoslavia, Europe was virtually free of armed conflict by 1996.

Figure 2.1 illustrates world trends in the occurrence of armed conflict in the 1990s. A similar pattern applies for the severity of the armed conflict, with severity defined in terms of casualties and encompassing the continuum from minor armed conflict to intermediate armed conflict to war.[3] The upsurge in armed activity in Kosovo in 1998–99

---

[1]As used here, an *armed conflict* is "a contested incompatibility which concerns government and/or territory where the use of armed force between two parties, of which at least one is the government of a state, results in at least 25 battle-related deaths." This definition is used by SIPRI (the Stockholm International Peace Research Institute) and other institutions monitoring conflict worldwide. (Peter Wallensteen and Margareta Sollenberg, "Armed Conflict, 1989-99," *Journal of Peace Research*, 37:5, 2000, p. 648.)

[2]These data are based on information published by the conflict monitoring group at Uppsala, which is used by SIPRI. For purposes of incidence of conflict, the Uppsala conflict monitoring group uses the following geographical delineation of the world into continents and regions: Europe (including the states of the Caucasus), Middle East (Egypt and southwestern Asia, including Turkey, Iran, and the Arabian peninsula), Asia (including Australia and Oceania), Africa (excluding Egypt), and the Americas (Western Hemisphere excluding the Pacific island states). (Wallensteen and Sollenberg, p. 648.)

[3]The data are from information published by the conflict monitoring group at Uppsala, which is used by SIPRI. The Uppsala group and SIPRI use the following definitions: *Minor armed conflict* is at least 25 battle-related deaths per year and fewer than 1,000 battle-related deaths during the course of the conflict. *Intermediate armed conflict* is at least 25 battle-related deaths per year and an accumulated total of at least 1,000 deaths, but fewer than 1,000 per year. *War* is at least 1,000 battle-related deaths per year. (Wallensteen and Sollenberg, p. 648.) According to the SIPRI definitions, there have been six European wars in the decade of the 1990s (Bosnia-Herzegovina, Croatia, Kosovo, Chechnya, Georgia, and Azerbaijan), but the inclusion of wars in the Caucasus (Chechnya, Georgia, and Azerbaijan) within this European category is questionable. In standard geographical definitions of Europe, the south Caucasus forms a part of Asia: "On east, the conventional boundary [of Europe with Asia is] . . . Ural Mountains and Ural River; on southeast, Caspian Sea; on south, Caucasus

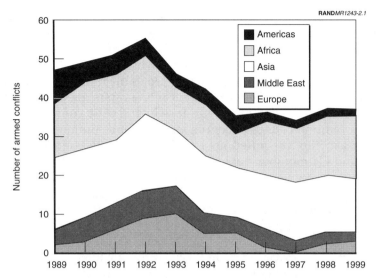

Figure 2.1—Number of Armed Conflicts by Region, 1989–99

that led to NATO's Operation Allied Force against Yugoslavia in 1999 does not alter either pattern significantly. Furthermore, the near-term potential for a major inter-state war in Europe is currently low[4]—in marked contrast to the high potential for a major war that characterized the Cold War—and this situation is not likely to change unless Europe undergoes a major shock equal in magnitude to the fall of communism.

The benign security environment does not mean, however, that there are no disputes. Some territorial-, resource-, and minority-related

---

Mountains, Black Sea, and Mediterranean. . . . [Europe is separated] from Turkey in Asia by Dardanelles, Sea of Marmara, and Bosporus." (*Merriam-Webster's Geographical Dictionary*, Merriam-Webster, Inc., Springfield, MA, 1997.) Reassigning two of the Caucasian conflicts (Georgia and Azerbaijan) to the Asian or Middle Eastern category would reduce further the comparative severity and frequency of the armed conflicts in Europe in the 1990s.

[4]This is quite apart from the general evolution in conflict trends, in which the overwhelming majority of armed conflict in the world is intra-state rather than inter-state. According to data assembled by the Uppsala group, out of the 110 armed conflicts that took place in 1989–99, only seven (6 percent) were inter-state. Of the rest, 94 were intra-state, and nine were intra-state with foreign intervention. (Wallensteen and Sollenberg, p. 639.)

inter-state tensions persist in Europe. So far, a multitude of conflict resolution and conflict management mechanisms have prevented such disputes and tensions from escalating to militarized strife (with the prominent exception of the former Yugoslavia), and they reasonably may be expected to continue to do so in the future. The potential for conflict, mainly internal but also inter-state, exists primarily in the "unintegrated" area of Europe, which mostly consists of formerly communist states in central, eastern, and southern Europe.[5] In contrast, the integrated area of Europe, consisting roughly of NATO and EU member states, has achieved a high level of political and economic integration leading to a true "security community"—a region in which war has ceased to be an option for solving disputes between members. In such a context, peace operations in the unintegrated area of Europe—ranging from coercive peace enforcement (such as NATO's Kosovo operation in 1999) to less contested forms (such as NATO's involvement in Bosnia-Herzegovina)—are the most likely military operations that NATO would undertake in the near- or mid-term.

The benign security environment represents a complete change from what had been the "natural" state of affairs in Europe in the modern era (and even earlier), one characterized by frequent major wars and near-war crises. The major difference between the post–World War II situation and the historical pattern is that the United States, through its creation of NATO and its preponderant position within NATO, denationalized defense in the part of Europe outside the Soviet zone of control. This military unity that the United States imposed on the main European states (except Russia) through NATO then allowed political and economic unity to develop and to evolve all the way to the current stage of a security community.

Presently, the United States, and the U.S.-led alliance, has a preponderance of power in Europe, and nothing on the horizon indicates a serious challenge to that preponderance.[6] Although causality is im-

---

[5]Vladimir Tismaneanu, *Nationalism, Populism, and Other Threats to Liberal Democracy in Post-Communist Europe*, The Donald W. Treadgold Papers in Russian, East European, and Central Asian Studies, No. 20, January 1999, The Henry M. Jackson School of International Studies, The University of Washington, Seattle.

[6]Despite much writing in the early 1990s that the unipolar (U.S.-dominant) situation in the world amounted to a temporary stage, reality has shown otherwise, with a

possible to prove conclusively, the creation of a benign security environment in Europe as a whole (not just in the integrated portion) in the second half of the 1990s is at least correlated with NATO's preponderance of power in Europe and its transformation from an organization focused primarily on collective defense of member states into a mechanism for conflict prevention and conflict management in areas outside the NATO member states. It is hypothesized here that NATO's self-designation as an institution for upholding peace and security in Europe and its proven willingness to use force for conflict management and conflict prevention in areas outside NATO member states have played a major role in bringing about the currently existing benign security environment in Europe, for NATO's actions have meant that leaders in the unintegrated part of Europe who otherwise might have used force to pursue their goals have had to modify their behavior to take NATO's potential reaction into account.

The security environment is currently being further shaped by NATO's enlargement strategy, which serves to impose a behavioral regime on much of unintegrated Europe. Countries in this region have the possibility of full membership or a privileged cooperative status if they abide by a set of norms meant to advance democratic internal development and cooperative international behavior. The linkage between a country's behavior and its suitability for NATO membership represents a complete switch from the way NATO enlarged during the Cold War. NATO's commitment to enlargement, demonstrated by the admission of three new members in 1999, has provided leaders in this region with incentives to pursue reform and to settle disputes with neighboring countries.

Put bluntly, NATO's current strategy resembles the proverbial carrot and stick. NATO's enlargement offers the inducement of membership (the carrot) as a way to encourage peaceful transformation and integration into a larger European security community. NATO's transformation, into a conflict prevention and management organi-

---

decade of U.S. preponderance of power and no competitor in sight in the short- or mid-term. There are convincing arguments that, failing a major U.S. blunder, the "unipolar moment" is here to stay for the foreseeable future. (William C. Wohlforth, "The Stability of a Unipolar World," *International Security*, 24:1, Summer 1999, pp. 5–41; David A. Lake, "Ulysses's Triumph: American Power and the New World Order, *Security Studies*, 8:4, Summer 1999, pp. 44–78.)

zation, provides the coercive component (the stick) that can be used to enforce peace and deter aggression in and around Europe.

NATO'S TRANSFORMATION

NATO's emphasis on collective and cooperative security is the core of its continued relevance in contemporary Europe. NATO's transformation is not a fundamental reorientation, since NATO has always had elements of collective security and a vision of lasting and peaceful order in Europe based on democratic political systems and shared security.[7] But during the Cold War, the presence of a clear external military threat to NATO member states made NATO's collective security elements secondary to its deterrence and warfighting roles. The end of the Cold War brought a series of NATO decisions, beginning in London (1990) and culminating in Brussels (1994), through which NATO moved to downplay its warfighting elements and instead emphasize its collective security elements. NATO's agenda now includes conflict prevention and, in the words of NATO's 1991 Strategic Concept, promotion of a "zone of stability and security" in and around Europe.[8] NATO's current role is illustrated by its involvement in the former Yugoslavia since 1993, which has emphasized peacekeeping and peace enforcement while retaining, in a residual form, the traditional mission of deterring potential military threats to NATO members. In short, to remain relevant and continue to play a role in shaping European security, NATO reinvented itself in the 1990s as an institution for dealing with the perceived security problems in contemporary Europe.

The transformation serves U.S. interests in that NATO remains the primary mechanism for a U.S. leadership role in European security. As such, NATO gives the United States a means of influencing the security evolution in Europe and enhancing the U.S. ability to project power to other areas important to the U.S. national interest, such as

---

[7]NATO's founding document, the Washington Treaty, has specific language along these lines. Numerous NATO documents throughout NATO's Cold War history (for example, the Harmel Report) also made references to NATO's non-military goals. For a discussion of collective security and NATO, see David S. Yost, "The New NATO and Collective Security," *Survival*, 40:2, Summer 1998, pp. 135–160.

[8]For the text of NATO's 1991 Strategic Concept, see http://www.nato.int/docu/basics.htm.

the Middle East. Moreover, NATO does all of the above not by way of a domineering hegemonic application of U.S. power, but in the context of a mutually beneficial mechanism that serves the interests of all NATO members.

The new orientation has been given expression in NATO's 1991 and 1999 Strategic Concepts. Each of these represents a culmination of years of negotiation among members on NATO's direction. Absent a major political shock that would revolutionize the security environment, the fundamental course for NATO's role and evolution in the Europe of the early 21st century is in place. Complex organizations with a multitude of members and an emphasis on consensus do not change course easily. Having chosen to be an instrument of peacekeeping and conflict prevention, NATO is likely to persist in emphasizing its collective security role for the foreseeable future. Some setbacks in implementing this role may lead to a reexamination of the tactics, but only repeated setbacks are likely to lead to a reexamination of the strategy itself.

This is not to say that the collective defense aspects of NATO will go away. For one, these aspects play a conflict-preventing role by keeping the security community intact and by deterring the emergence of potential challenges to NATO. But these aspects also play a crucial role in NATO's peace operations. Almost paradoxically, the collective defense core will remain essential to providing the deterrent and the military muscle needed to make NATO peace enforcement and peacekeeping effective. NATO's integrated command arrangements, its common procedures and doctrine, and the trust and bonds developed over decades of cooperation are an irreplaceable force multiplier, and if coercive application of power is needed, they will ensure that the requisite military capabilities are provided in a politically effective multinational fashion.

NATO's Current Strategic Concept

The 1999 Strategic Concept provides the institutional justification and direction for NATO's further development and is likely to remain the main blueprint for NATO's evolution during the next 10 to 15 years. The Concept identifies the security of member states in a broad fashion, seeing it as being potentially at risk from "crisis and conflict . . . [that can affect] the Euro-Atlantic area."[9]   According to the Concept, a variety of internal problems in countries that are not NATO members could present potential NATO security threats:

> The security of the Alliance remains subject to a wide variety of military and non-military risks which are multi-directional and often difficult to predict. These risks include uncertainty and instability in and around the Euro-Atlantic area and the possibility of regional crises at the periphery of the Alliance, which could evolve rapidly. Some countries in and around the Euro-Atlantic area face serious economic, social and political difficulties. Ethnic and religious rivalries, territorial disputes, inadequate or failed efforts at reform, the abuse of human rights, and the dissolution of states can lead to local and even regional instability. The resulting tensions could lead to crises affecting Euro-Atlantic stability, to human suffering, and to armed conflicts. Such conflicts could affect the security of the Alliance by spilling over into neighbouring countries, including NATO countries, or in other ways, and could also affect the security of other states.[10]

The presence of nuclear arsenals; the global proliferation of nuclear, biological, and chemical weapons; and the spread of advanced weapon technologies in general are also significant NATO concerns.[11]

The 1999 Strategic Concept clearly states that actions short of a military attack on a NATO member can trigger a NATO response:

> Alliance security interests can be affected by other risks of a wider nature, including acts of terrorism, sabotage and organized crime, and by the disruption of the flow of vital resources. The uncontrolled movement of large numbers of people, particularly as a consequence of armed conflicts, can also pose problems for security and stability affecting the Alliance.[12]

---

[9]*The Alliance's Strategic Concept,* April 24, 1999, paragraph 6; http://www.nato.int/docu/pr/1999/p99-065e.htm.

[10]Ibid., paragraph 20.

[11]Ibid., paragraphs 21–23.

[12]Ibid., paragraph 24.

In support of NATO's residual collective defense function, the Concept justifies the continued need for NATO in terms of the potential for a long-term emergence of a military challenger. Although the Concept does not mention any country explicitly, Russia is the most plausible (if not the only) candidate for such a role:

> Notwithstanding positive developments in the strategic environment and the fact that large-scale conventional aggression against the Alliance is highly unlikely, the possibility of such a threat emerging over the longer term exists.[13]

The broad definition of security threats does not mean that NATO will react militarily to every conceivable internal problem in a nonmember country in Europe, western Asia, or northern Africa. However, the Concept does justify and explain the process for addressing such issues and gives NATO the prerogative to decide whether to act. By combining a broad definition of security with a linkage between the security of partner (i.e., non-member) states and that of member states, NATO has assigned to itself an all-encompassing mandate in the security realm in and around Europe.

The relevance of a document such as the 1999 Strategic Concept to dealing with a particular crisis is indirect. In the event of an actual crisis, the political decisions made in the major NATO capitals—not simply the Concept—will determine whether and how NATO reacts. However, the Concept effectively limits the choices available to the major member states for responding to crises; it has, in other words, a "tying of hands" effect. Having established a specific set of tasks and concerns for itself, NATO must deal with these adequately if it is to maintain credibility. Thus, military threats to a NATO partner state, cases of armed reprisals against minority populations in a state near NATO, and even the existence on NATO's periphery of weak states with corrupt regimes and a prominent role for organized crime—all of these amount to security issues of concern to NATO, as defined by NATO itself.

---

[13]Ibid., paragraph 20.

Problems in NATO's Transformation

NATO's transformation has raised questions about the appropriateness of a military alliance reorienting itself to project power for purposes of conflict prevention and conflict management outside its member states. Most of all, the transformation has heightened NATO's collective action problem. The secondary and discretionary nature of security threats that lead to peace operations provides an incentive for individual members to "free ride" (contribute nothing) or "easy ride" (contribute little) in NATO peace operations, leaving other members to take on bigger roles (and costs).[14] This collective action problem is not new, but in its current manifestation, it is more acute and troubling. For an organization such as NATO, which acts on the basis of consensus and trust and relies for its effectiveness on the foundation of a collective defense commitment, the greater incentives to free or easy ride call into question NATO's long-term viability and cohesiveness.[15] Moreover, NATO's adversaries are bound to exploit the more acute elements of the collective action problem.[16]

Through its transformation, NATO has adapted to the new security environment in Europe and has remained not only relevant but dominant in the realm of European security. However, in the course of its adaptation, NATO has put at risk some of the essential characteristics that underpinned its effectiveness for four decades. The heightened collective action problem does not necessarily mean that the transformation was a poor strategic choice for the United States, since the alternative—refusing to adapt to the new strategic environment—might have led to NATO's eventual demise[17] and, even

---

[14]Joseph Lepgold, "NATO's Post–Cold War Collective Action Problem," *International Security*, 23:1, Summer 1998, pp. 78–106.

[15]Todd Sandler, "The Future Challenges of NATO: An Economic Viewpoint," *Defence and Peace Economics*, 8:4, 1997, pp. 319–353; Joanne Wright, "Trusting Flexible Friends: The Dangers of Flexibility in NATO and the West European Union/European Union," *Contemporary Security Policy*," 20:1, April 1999, pp. 111–129.

[16]Barry Posen has argued that Milosevic's strategy during NATO's Kosovo operation was precisely along these lines. That the strategy failed this time does not mean it will fail the next time. (Barry R. Posen, "The War for Kosovo: Serbia's Political-Military Strategy," *International Security*, 24:4, Spring 2000, pp. 39–84.)

[17]However, the claim that NATO surely would have fallen apart had it not transformed itself (in other words, that NATO faced a choice of "transform or perish") is not borne

more important, to a smaller U.S. role in shaping the European security environment. The path of transformation has been chosen; NATO will need to prove that it can overcome its acute collective action problem.

NATO'S ENLARGEMENT

The process leading up to an enlargement decision involves multiple complexities, especially in relation to the criteria used to select new members. Moreover, from a defense planning standpoint, NATO's specific enlargement strategy and process present further complications, some of which are inherent to the vision of an enlarged alliance. These two topics are addressed here in turn.

Enlargement is a complementary, rather than a necessary, component of NATO's post–Cold War transformation. Just as NATO has adopted many collective security elements in order to deter conflicts in areas on its periphery, so too has it set on a course of enlargement in order to institutionalize democratic and market reforms in the unintegrated areas of central, eastern, and southern Europe and thereby increase overall security. Enlargement is thus best seen analytically in terms of its intended role in shaping the security environment in Europe.[18]

In this sense, enlargement capitalizes on NATO's attraction for many former communist states by establishing a set of behavioral incentives for new and prospective members' domestic and foreign policies. Upon evidence of a country's institutionalization of NATO's membership criteria (or, in other words, completion of the transition process), NATO—in theory—will offer full membership and integration. The enlargement study that NATO issued in 1995 introduced a

---

out by empirical studies of alliance duration. (D. Scott Bennett, "Testing Alternative Models of Alliance Duration, 1816–1984," *American Journal of Political Science*, 41:3, July 1997, pp. 846–878.)

[18]Traditional (threat-based) explanations for alliance formation fail to explain NATO's post–Cold War enlargement. Explanations based on the "socialization" function of the enlargement process come closest to capturing its shaping intent. (Lars S. Skalnes, "From the Outside In, from the Inside Out: NATO Expansion and International Relations Theory," *Security Studies*, 7:4, Summer 1998, pp. 44–87; Frank Schimmelfennig, "NATO Enlargement: A Constructivist Explanation," *Security Studies*, 8:2–3, Winter 1998/99–Spring 1999, pp. 198–234.)

host of criteria that prospective members are to meet prior to accession, including the following main conditions:

1. A functioning democratic political system (including free and fair elections and respect for individual liberty and the rule of law) and a market economy.

2. Democratic-style civil-military relations.

3. Treatment of minority populations in accordance with Organization for Security and Cooperation in Europe (OSCE) guidelines.

4. Resolution of disputes with neighboring countries and a commitment to solving international disputes peacefully.

5. A military contribution to the alliance and a willingness to take steps to achieve interoperability with other alliance members.[19]

To ensure that new members do not use NATO membership to gain advantages in bilateral relations with neighbors, NATO requires new members to commit themselves to keeping the door open to further enlargement.[20]

The fact that NATO has elaborated pre-accession criteria does not mean that a country is guaranteed accession by meeting all of them. NATO made clear that these criteria establish only the pre-conditions for consideration for membership and that the act of inviting a state to join ultimately remains a political decision to be made by NATO members:

> Decisions on enlargement will be for NATO itself. Enlargement will occur through a gradual, deliberate, and transparent process, encompassing dialogue with all interested parties. There is no fixed or rigid list of criteria for inviting new member states to join the Alliance. Enlargement will be decided on a case-by-case basis and some nations may attain membership before others. New members should not be admitted or excluded on the basis of belonging to some group or category. Ultimately, Allies will decide by consensus

---

[19] *Study on NATO Enlargement*, September 1995, paragraphs 4–7 and 70–78; http://www.nato.int/docu/basictxt/enl-9501.htm.

[20] Ibid., paragraph 30.

whether to invite each new member to join according to their judgement of whether doing so will contribute to security and stability in the North Atlantic area at the time such a decision is to be made.[21]

In effect, NATO is asking aspiring members to meet almost entirely non-military criteria just to be considered for admission. In other words, NATO is using the widely shared aspirations for long-term security of the former communist states to encourage those states to make the transition from authoritarianism and communist autarky to democracy with a market economy.

It is important to keep in mind that neither enlargement nor the use of political and shaping imperatives is new. Similar motivations were behind West Germany's accession to NATO in 1955 and Spain's in 1982. But the current, far-reaching pre-conditions imposed on new members stand in contrast to the Cold War era's lack of any conditions on new members (other than the consensus of existing members). They did not exist for rounds of enlargement (Greece, Turkey, West Germany, Spain, and East Germany[22]) that took place prior to NATO's publication of its enlargement study in 1995. NATO focused on collective defense during the Cold War, so the political imperatives behind enlargement were secondary to military considerations. In short, the Washington Treaty's Article 10 sufficed:

> The Parties may, by unanimous agreement, invite any other European State in a position to further the principles of this Treaty and to contribute to the security of the North Atlantic area to accede to this Treaty.

NATO's evolution toward a role entailing both cooperative and collective security means that political imperatives (an environment-shaping agenda of democratization and integration) and non-military stipulations are driving NATO's current enlargement. The pre-conditions NATO imposes on aspiring members lead to intense scrutiny of aspiring members' extent of compliance. Ironically, several long-standing members would certainly not meet the current

---

[21]Ibid., paragraph 7.

[22]The absorption of East Germany into NATO through the back door of German unification in 1990 represents a unique path to NATO enlargement.

criteria for admission (Greece and Turkey most of all, and possibly others).[23] Nothing indicates better NATO's transformation and shift in focus than the difference between the Cold War and post–Cold War criteria for and process of admission.

Reality of the 1997–99 Enlargement

NATO not only established pre-admission criteria for new members, it also reserved explicitly for itself the right to determine whether an aspiring member met the criteria. Interpreting how a country has fulfilled the criteria is a political process, one that was illustrated during the first round of post–Cold War enlargement in 1997–99. Although an enlargement decision is said to be based on consensus among all existing members, the preferences of the major NATO members carry more weight than those of the smaller members. Thus, in the run-up to the invitations issued at NATO's 1997 Madrid summit, the U.S. preference for issuing invitations only to Poland, the Czech Republic, and Hungary carried the day. In other words, although the pre-admission criteria provide a measure of transparency in decisionmaking concerning the enlargement process, their being met in no way guarantees accession.

Strategic considerations, though acknowledged only implicitly as a basis for admission in NATO's 1995 enlargement study, certainly played a role in the decision to invite Poland, the Czech Republic, and Hungary. U.S. interests in ensuring a successful transition in central Europe naturally focused on the largest and most-developed former communist countries closest to Germany, NATO's central core in Europe. The contiguity of pre-accession Poland and the Czech Republic with NATO, and especially Germany (a major NATO country and the other prime mover, besides the United States, for NATO's enlargement), influenced the decision to issue invitations to these two countries. Hungary, although not contiguous to a NATO country, had played an important role since 1995 in supporting NATO's conflict management and peace operations in former Yugoslavia. For Germany, the main interest in enlargement focused

---

[23]Both Greece and Turkey fail on the basis of resolving disputes with neighboring countries (each other, most of all); Turkey also would fail to pass the requirements of democracy and civil-military relations.

on countries to its immediate east, so as to eliminate its "eastern frontier" status in NATO and thus lower its security risks and costs.

Most observers and analysts recognized the three countries invited in 1997 as the most advanced of the former communist states in their transition and reform process, and there was widespread agreement that all three had largely met the pre-admission criteria. Nonetheless, in early 1997, NATO had reached consensus only on issuing an admission to Poland.[24] A few members remained uncommitted regarding the Czech Republic, primarily because of questions about its ability to contribute much (militarily or otherwise) to NATO. Hungary elicited even greater skepticism because of its minorities' problems with neighboring countries and its questionable potential for contributing militarily. The ultimate decision to issue invitations to the three countries emerged only after intense intra-alliance bargaining,[25] which even involved subjects not tied to enlargement, such as reorganization of NATO's command structure.[26]

Idiosyncratic considerations were also present in the decisionmaking process. Public opinion in support of specific countries differed in the various NATO member states. Such considerations included widespread sympathy for two of the countries, Poland and the Czech Republic, because of the tragic histories of their past 50 years. They also included sympathy for the anti-communist movements and/or uprisings in all three of the countries, perceptions of cultural similarities, and the existence of long-standing ties with these countries. While not central, such considerations constrained the debates in the major NATO countries and thus, at least indirectly, influenced the outcome.

---

[24]Author's conversation (March 1998) with a then (1997) high-ranking U.S. official to NATO. For an argument for and a detailed discussion of why only Poland deserved an invitation, see Vojtech Mastny, "Reassuring NATO: Eastern Europe, Russia, and the Western Alliance," *Forsvarsstudier* (Defense Studies), Norwegian Institute for Defense Studies, No. 5, 1997.

[25]All the southern European NATO countries, as well as a few others, supported the candidacy of Slovenia and Romania. This preference arose not necessarily from any expectation that Romania would be invited to join, but out of concerns that the enlargement focus was too northern and too German-centered.

[26]Author's conversations (March 1998, March 2000) with two U.S. officials then (1997) based at NATO.

As illustrated by this first round of enlargement, the pre-conditions for admission narrow down the field of potential candidates by eliminating countries that obviously do not qualify. But strategic considerations, alliance bargaining, and even idiosyncratic national preferences influence the decision to issue an invitation for membership to a specific country. It is impossible to ascertain quantitatively the importance of the various factors in the decisionmaking process, but it is important nonetheless to recognize that the process is essentially political—i.e., does not stem from a clear threat but, rather, is based on an environment-shaping agenda of democratization and integration—and that a variety of factors enter the decision calculus. The fact that non-military considerations dominate the decisionmaking process underscores the idea that enlargement, as currently conceived by NATO, is not a response to realist formulations of threat. Instead, it stems from NATO's transformation into a conflict management organization and a tool for the reintegration of Europe.

Implications of NATO's Enlargement Strategy

From the perspective of improving regional security and advancing democracy in the former communist states in central and southern Europe, the NATO enlargement process has had the desired effect.[27] For the new members, the pre-conditions formed an important motivation for signing the Hungarian-Romanian treaty (1997), the evolution in Polish civil-military relations that took place in 1996–97, and stepping up structural reforms in all three countries to make their armed forces more compatible with NATO. Even for the countries that aspired to join NATO but were not invited in 1997, the need to meet the pre-conditions has had the desired effect, as evidenced by Romania's signing of treaties with Ukraine and Hungary[28] and its

---

[27]This is not to say that NATO's system of incentives was the only one present: The EU's setting out of similar criteria for EU membership certainly contributed to the effect, and there were domestic pressures, varying in intensity depending on the country, in the same direction. But from the policy standpoint of the EU and NATO countries, the similar criteria established by EU and NATO amounted to two sides of the same coin and created a powerful incentive system in favor of advancing peaceful evolution and democratization in the unintegrated part of Europe.

[28]As one scholar put it, "When the theoretical possibility of membership [in NATO] changed to an achievable goal, the governments in Budapest and Bucharest modified

shift in how it treats ethnic Hungarians in Romania, as well as by Slovenia's increased attention to contributing militarily to NATO. Even in Slovakia, an aspiring country that NATO disqualified for failing to meet the pre-conditions, the missed invitation contributed to a backlash against leaders with authoritarian proclivities that then toppled them from power in the next elections.[29]

However, the shaping strategy underlying NATO's enlargement has two main complications. The first is the basic assumption that the behavioral regime imposed on a country by the pre-admission criteria will persist once that country becomes a NATO member. In other words, admission is tantamount to recognizing that the new member has institutionalized the reforms and no longer significantly differs from long-time members in its domestic practices and its foreign policy underpinnings. This assumption may not necessarily hold true. While it is still too soon to assess whether this assumption is valid for the three members that acceded to NATO in 1999, there are some indications of potential problems, at least in the case of Hungary. Hungary's defense spending, as measured by a percentage of gross domestic product (GDP), has remained low since its accession despite Hungary's pre-accession pledges to increase it.[30] Furthermore, unilateral Hungarian activism on behalf of Hungarian minorities in neighboring countries increased after accession—for example, the Hungarian prime minister linked the issue of ethnic Hungarians in Voivodina (northern Serbia) with a settlement in Kosovo in the immediate aftermath of Operation Allied Force. The first issue calls into question Hungary's commitment to making a contribution to NATO; the second introduces the uncomfortable

---

their behavior and recast their identities in line with the norms explicitly espoused by the group of Western states they wanted to join." (Ronald H. Linden, "Putting on Their Sunday Best: Romania, Hungary, and the Puzzle of Peace," *International Studies Quarterly*, 44:1, 2000, p. 137.)

[29]EU incentives also were important in Slovakia. See Geoffrey Pridham, "Complying with the European Union's Democratic Conditionality: Transnational Party Linkages and Regime Change in Slovakia, 1993–1998, *Europe-Asia Studies*, 51:7, 1999, pp. 1221–1244.

[30]Hungary agreed to raise its defense spending to 1.8 percent of GDP by 2001, which is still well below the 2.0 percent median in NATO. Depending on the method of calculation used, Hungary's defense budget is either slightly (1.7 percent, according to official NATO figures) or substantially (1.3 percent, according to SIPRI) below the targeted level. This issue is covered in more depth in the next chapter.

question of whether Hungary is using NATO to advance its perceived national goals in a bilateral dispute.

The other and potentially more important complication with respect to the shaping strategy is the divergence between NATO's need to engage Russia and the historically understandable concerns about Russia that many of the aspiring members have. NATO's motivations for enlargement stem not from a perceived Russian threat, but from a desire to reintegrate Europe and to establish an incentive structure for the former communist states of Europe to encourage them to undertake internal reforms that will lead to a more democratic and secure continent. Although NATO's 1999 Strategic Concept retains language implying some concern about the potential for Russia to threaten Europe militarily, NATO has gone to great lengths to engage Russia in military cooperation and partnership to ensure that the concerns do not come to fruition.

Russia has cooperated with NATO, albeit reluctantly, but opposes NATO's enlargement and transformation. This opposition stems from various causes. Many in the Russian foreign policy elite have not reconciled themselves to the loss of empire and drop in international status and maintain a deep-seated "enemy image" of NATO that is rooted in the four decades of the Cold War. In addition, a persistence of zero-sum thinking and either a lack of understanding or a mistrust of the extent of NATO's post–Cold War transformation have led to the Russian perception that NATO's enlargement and preeminence in Europe (combined with the low likelihood that Russia will be able to join NATO) will keep Russia from playing a role in European security. NATO's "encroachment" into Slavic-inhabited areas has concerned Russians who feel they have special rights in these countries or who think in terms of "civilizational conflict"; other Russians fear that the issue of NATO will dominate Russia's relations with the major NATO countries, thereby detracting from the cause of reform in Russia.[31] Although opinion polls have consis-

---

[31]For insightful analyses of the various foreign policy schools in Russia and their rationale for opposition to NATO's enlargement, see Alexander A. Sergounin, "Russian Domestic Debate on NATO Enlargement: From Phobia to Damage Limitation," *European Security*, 6:4, Winter 1997, pp. 55–71; Vladimir Shlapentokh, "'Old,' 'New' and 'Post' Liberal Attitudes Toward the West: From Love to Hate," *Communist and Post-Communist Studies*, 31:3, September 1998, pp. 199–216.

tently shown that the Russian public does not see NATO enlargement as a threat or even as an important issue, Russian elites across the political spectrum, for a variety of reasons, have been largely united in viewing NATO enlargement as non-beneficial to Russia.[32]

The need to engage Russia, largely seen as important by NATO's Cold War–era members, is much less popular among the former communist states aspiring to become members, according to public opinion surveys.[33] These states aspire to NATO membership because they see it as a way to ensure their long-term security, as a political expression of their sense of "civilizational" belonging, and as an official stamp of approval for their transition process. This is especially true of states that were formerly satellites of the USSR and thus have emerged only recently from five decades of direct foreign domination or foreign-imposed authoritarian regimes. Moreover, those countries that were under foreign-imposed regimes were forced to pursue economic and social policies that, often for the first time in history, differentiated them from what are now considered their "Western" neighbors.[34] When the 50 years of foreign domination is viewed as a five-decade interruption of their "normal" political and economic development, it is not surprising that both the elites and the general publics in these countries have greater concern for long-term security than do those in long-standing NATO states. They view

---

[32]It is important to note that it was NATO's war over Kosovo that galvanized Russian public opinion against NATO, something that discussions of NATO enlargement could not do for several years. (Vladimir Shlapentokh, "The Balkan War, the Rise of Anti-Americanism and the Future of Democracy in Russia," *International Journal of Public Opinion Research*, 11:3, Fall 1999, pp. 275–288.)

[33]Tatiana Kostadinova, "East European Public Support for NATO Membership: Fears and Aspirations," *Journal of Peace Research*, 37:2, 2000, pp. 235–249.

[34]For example, prior to World War II, the standard of living was higher in the Czech lands than in Austria, Estonia was at a level of development similar to Finland's, and Bulgaria and Greece were at a similar level. Moreover, these pairs of countries shared a common history and experienced no "Western" vs. "Eastern" differences prior to Soviet domination. While catching up will be hampered by the large differences in levels of affluence between the former communist states and the wealthy EU countries, the progress made already by "star pupils," such as Poland and Estonia, shows that with proper political conditions in place, the former communist states can make up lost ground quickly. Economic projections show that at least some of the central European states have the potential to be at the then EU average levels of affluence (as measured by per capita output) by 2030. (Andrzej Brzeski and Enrico Colombatto, "Can Eastern Europe Catch Up?" *Post-Communist Economies*, 11:1, March 1999, pp. 5–26.)

NATO membership as righting a historical wrong and as a major step in integrating into the "West" and erasing the 50 years of differences that arose between them and their neighbors outside the communist autarkic model. Quite aside from the specific impact of this lengthy communist rule, these states have limited experience with full national sovereignty in the modern era. This too leads to greater concern with security than is exhibited by NATO countries that have been secure for decades.

Other than Albania and the states of former Yugoslavia (which tend to focus on security threats from each other), the former communist states aspiring to NATO membership are more concerned about the possible reappearance of a security threat from Russia than are the long-standing NATO states. In countries whose history of conflict with Russia pre-dates World War II, security concerns are magnified. Although perceptions of a potential Russian threat in the near- or mid-term exist only perhaps in Lithuania, Latvia, and Estonia (which lost their sovereignty altogether and were forcibly annexed to the USSR for over four decades) or in Ukraine, general concern about the long-term prospects of the transition going on in Russia, nervousness over the unpredictability of the Russian evolution, and general wariness regarding the consequences if the Russian transition were to falter are shared by all the former communist states. Most U.S. analysts share the attitude of caution and uncertainty toward Russia's evolution into a democratic country,[35] and these views are

---

[35]Along with China, Cuba, Iran, and North Korea, Russia is one of the five countries identified as "strategic priorities" for monitoring by the U.S. intelligence community (Director of Central Intelligence, "Annual Report for the United States Intelligence Community [1999]," May 2000; http://www.odci.gov/cia/publications/fy99intellrpt/dci_annual_report_99.html). For analyses of impediments to a Russian transition to a democracy, see Harry Eckstein, Frederic J. Fleron, Jr., Erik P. Hoffmann, and William M. Reisinger, with Richard Ahl, Russell Bova, and Philip G. Roeder, *Can Democracy Take Root in Post-Soviet Russia? Explorations in State-Society Relations*, Lanham, MD: Rowman and Littlefield Publishers, 1998; James L. Gibson, "Putting Up with Fellow Russians: An Analysis of Political Tolerance in the Fledgling Russian Democracy," *Political Research Quarterly*, 51:1, March 1998, pp. 37–68; M. Steven Fish, *Democracy from Scratch: Opposition and Regime in the New Russian Revolution*, Princeton: Princeton University Press, 1995; Michael McFaul, "Russia's 'Privatized' State as an Impediment to Democratic Consolidation," *Security Dialogue*, 29:2, June 1998, pp. 191–199 (part 1), and 29:3, September 1998 (part 2), pp. 315–332; John B. Dunlop, "Sifting Through the Rubble of the Yeltsin Years," *Problems of Post-Communism*, 47:1, January–February 2000, pp. 3–15; Amy Knight, *The Security Services and the Decline of Democracy in Russia: 1996–1999*, The Donald W. Treadgold Papers in Russian, East

evident in the hedging elements in U.S. policy toward Russia. However, such concerns are magnified in the former communist states because of their proximity and their historical experiences during the 20th century.[36]

The effect of these perceptions of insecurity has been to make the former communist states of Europe generally less interested in or understanding of NATO's post–Cold War transformation. In the words of a former deputy chief of the Polish mission to NATO:

> Speaking honestly, we have rather mixed feelings [concerning the 1999 Strategic Concept], because we really would like to enjoy membership in "traditional" NATO. For half a century, we in Poland were denied stability and security that was enjoyed, for example, in the U.S. At least for a few years we would like to enjoy peace and security and simply feel confident under the nuclear umbrella. But it has turned out that immediately after accession to the alliance we had to begin discussing seriously the changes within and the transformation of the alliance. Many politicians [in Poland] do not like such a situation. The reason is understandable, for we would like to have a feeling of peace and security and we did not want to enter an organization in the midst of a metamorphosis.[37]

European, and Central Asian Studies, No. 23, October 1999, The Henry M. Jackson School of International Studies, The University of Washington, Seattle; Stephen E. Hanson and Jeffrey S. Kopstein, "The Weimar/Russia Comparison," *Post-Soviet Affairs*, 13:3, July 1997, pp. 252–283. There is even a continuing debate on the prospects for Russia's disintegration: Thomas E. Graham, "The Prospect of Russian Disintegration Is Low," *European Security*, 8:2, Summer 1999, pp. 1–14; Graeme P. Herd, "Russia: Systemic Transformation or Federal Collapse?" *Journal of Peace Research*, 36:3, May 1999, pp. 259–269; Robert J. Kaiser, "Prospects for the Disintegration of the Russian Federation," *Post-Soviet Geography*, 36:7, September 1995, pp. 426–435.

[36]None of the above is meant to downplay the security concerns of the states bordering Russia, since Russian nationalists have explicitly expansionist aims. But NATO's power preponderance and the limited inroads by militant Russian nationalists in the Russian parliament mean that expansionist aims are not an immediate problem. (Tuomas Forsberg, ed., *Contested Territory: Border Disputes at the Edge of the Former Soviet Empire*, Aldershot: Edward Elgar, 1995; Yury Polsky, "Russian Nationalists' Worldview," *The Soviet and Post-Soviet Review*, 23:1, 1998, pp. 107–119; Stephen D. Shenfield, *Russian Fascism: Traditions, Tendencies, Movements*, New York: M. E. Sharpe, 2000; Vera Tolz, "Conflicting 'Homeland Myths' and Nation-State Building in Postcommunist Russia," *Slavic Review*, 57:2, Summer 1998, pp. 267–294.)

[37]Comments made by Witold Waszczykowski at a round-table discussion at the Euro-Atlantic Association, Warsaw, April 9, 1999, as transcribed in "NATO-Nowe Wyzwania" (NATO—New Challenges), *Polska w Europie*, No. 29, August 1999, p. 74.

The elites and publics in some of the aspiring member countries wish to join the "old" NATO; some even see NATO's transformation as window dressing for its "real" (i.e., anti-Russian) functions. While they do not necessarily see a military threat to their countries in the near- or mid-term, they do see NATO's collective defense function as crucial to their long-term security. Ironically, such views parallel the Russian skepticism toward NATO's transformation. The divergence in motivations between the new and aspiring members and most of the Cold War–era members has implications for the adherence of new members to NATO's strategy for engaging Russia and for the participation of new and potential members in NATO conflict management efforts and peace operations. It will not be easy for NATO to square aspiring members' (historically understandable) concerns about Russia with NATO's need to engage Russia in cooperative relations and partnership.

DEGREES OF NATO COMMITMENT

NATO's transformation into an institution with more collective security functions and its diminishment of the sharp differences between Article 5 and Article 4 missions have created complications for defense planning. By defining security in more-inclusive terms, closely linking the security of NATO members with the security of non-members in Europe, and explicitly denoting some countries as future members, NATO has intentionally blurred the line dividing members and non-members. The basic, treaty-stipulated distinction between the U.S. commitment to "alliance members" and the U.S. commitment to "close partners" remains, but because of NATO's transformation, the United States now may be seen as having extended an implicit security guarantee to many non-member states. The degree of this implicit NATO security guarantee varies with the level of interdependence established with NATO countries through membership in the EU, as well as with geography and the likelihood of future NATO membership. What this all means is that there are now "gray areas" of commitment and thus future-planning uncertainties, such as what roles specific partner countries are to play in NATO and in NATO's potential operations.

The nature of the gray-area commitment relates to a country's membership in a NATO "outreach" entity, the EU, or the OSCE. There are three outreach entities. One of them, the Euro-Atlantic Partnership Council (EAPC), is a consultative body set up as a forum for deliberations on security issues in Europe and former Soviet space; another, Partnership for Peace (PfP), is a military cooperation program between NATO and non-NATO countries. In makeup, the memberships of EAPC and PfP (coterminous with the exception of Tajikistan) are similar to the membership of the OSCE, which is the most inclusive organization devoted to European security. Membership in EAPC and PfP is open to all European (and former Soviet) countries that adhere to basic UN principles of inter-state relations and wish to cooperate with NATO. PfP states that are singled out by NATO as possible future NATO members are allowed to engage in a regular set of interactions and receive assistance through the third outreach entity, the Membership Action Plan (MAP).

EU membership is largely coterminous with that of NATO Europe and, in practice, grants non-NATO countries a virtual presence in NATO through what is a deep level of political and economic integration with the NATO Europe states. Table 2.1 lists the memberships of the European countries in the various security-related institutions as of November 2000.

Categorization of Commitments

The member states of NATO and EU and the states on track to membership in the two institutions (based on EU's invitations in 1997 and 1999, and NATO's establishment of MAP in 1999) form the outlines of what, according to current consensus among EU and NATO members, a "united Europe" might look like at some indeterminate point in the future (see Figure 2.2). There are some oddities—the isolated Switzerland, Russia's Kaliningrad enclave, NATO protectorates over the proto-state Bosnia-Herzegovina and non-state Kosovo, and, until recently, the pariah state FR Yugoslavia (Serbia)—but the overall outlines are clear. Other than Lithuania, Latvia, and Estonia, the vision of a unified Europe stops at the former Soviet border. While NATO has attempted to engage and reassure Ukraine so as not to magnify its sense of vulnerability at being outside this area, the line's clarity is stark from the perspective of which European countries are and are not on track to membership in Europe's main security and political-economic organizations.

Table 2.1

European Membership in Main Security-Related Institutions

	NATO	EU	EU Future[a]	MAP	EAPC/ PfP[b]	OSCE[b]
Belgium	X	X			X	X
Czech Republic	X		X		X	X
Denmark	X	X			X	X
France	X	X			X	X
Germany	X	X			X	X
Greece	X	X			X	X
Hungary	X		X		X	X
Iceland	X				X	X
Italy	X	X			X	X
Luxembourg	X	X			X	X
Netherlands	X	X			X	X
Norway	X				X	X
Poland	X		X		X	X
Portugal	X	X			X	X
Spain	X	X			X	X
Turkey	X		XX		X	X
United Kingdom	X	X			X	X
Austria		X			X	X
Finland		X			X	X
Ireland		X			X	X
Sweden		X			X	X
Albania				X	X	X
Bulgaria			XX	X	X	X
Estonia			X	X	X	X
Latvia			XX	X	X	X
Lithuania			XX	X	X	X
Macedonia				X	X	X
Romania			XX	X	X	X
Slovakia			XX	X	X	X
Slovenia			X	X	X	X
Belarus					X	X
Croatia					X	X
Moldova					X	X
Russia					X	X
Switzerland					X	X
Ukraine					X	X
Bosnia-Herzegovina						X
FR Yugoslavia						X
Others[c]						X

[a]In this column, X = invited to EU accession talks in 1997; XX = invited to EU accession talks in 1999.

[b]EAPC, PfP, and OSCE also include the two North American NATO members (United States and Canada) and the post-Soviet states in Asia: Armenia, Azerbaijan, Georgia, Kazakhstan, Kyrgyzstan, Tajikistan (EAPC only), Turkmenistan, and Uzbekistan.

[c]Andorra, Cyprus, Holy See, Liechtenstein, Malta, Monaco, and San Marino.

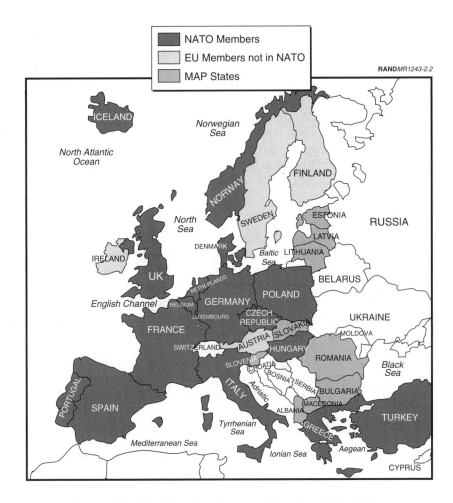

**Figure 2.2—Map Showing European Membership in Main
Security-Related Institutions**

It is important to keep in mind that placing a country on track to
NATO membership (i.e., in MAP) is only the expression of a commitment. The rationale that gives rise to this expression is the perception that the country will be part of a "future integrated Europe."
Thus, for example, because there is a consensus opinion among EU
members that Latvia is part of the vision of the "united Europe" being constructed by the EU, and because the EU and NATO have

agreed to keep membership in the two organizations largely coter-minus, NATO sees its security interests closely intertwined with those of Latvia. This has led to Latvia's being placed in MAP, and MAP is simply a mechanism for preparing Latvia for accession to NATO at some indeterminate point in the future. If a threat to Latvia were to develop prior to Latvia's becoming a NATO member, then, subject to the specific circumstances and nature of the threat, NATO would be likely to assist Latvia. The very act of putting a country on track to NATO membership is meant to deter threats from arising in the first place. The more explicit the guarantee, the greater the like-lihood that the commitment will be met; the very knowledge of this fact serves as a deterrent to the rise of threats.[38]

The vision of a unified Europe amounts to a major delineation of NATO's gray-area commitments. The differences between these commitments can be categorized, with differentiation based on the degree of integration with current NATO members. Figure 2.3 shows how the different levels of commitment overlap in terms of member-ship; Figure 2.4 illustrates the decreasing levels of NATO security commitments to members of the various institutions.

In Figure 2.4, the first group, or innermost area, is formed just by NATO members and thus is not a gray area: A clear, treaty-bound U.S. commitment to collective defense constitutes the basis for planning requirements in this area. This commitment entails proper preparation for the collective defense contingency, no matter how unlikely such a contingency currently may appear. Since the U.S. commitment to the Cold War–era NATO members has been demon-strated over five decades, it now requires mostly the continuation of

---

[38]The underlying principle is one of "audience costs," meaning that leaders in the democratic states that make up NATO's membership face great domestic pressures (and suffer major costs) if they do not honor international commitments. Consequently, democratic leaders have incentives to honor such commitments and can be expected to do so more than leaders in non-democratic countries, where open political discourse is proscribed. (James D. Fearon, "Domestic Political Audiences and the Escalation of International Disputes," *American Political Science Review*, 88:3, September 1994, pp. 577–592; Alastair Smith, "International Crises and Domestic Politics," *American Political Science Review*, 92:3, September 1998, pp. 623–638. For validation of Fearon's model of domestic audience costs, see Peter J. Partell and Glenn Palmer, "Audience Costs and Interstate Crises: An Empirical Assessment of Fearon's Model of Dispute Outcomes," *International Studies Quarterly*, 43:2, June 1999, pp. 389–405.)

regular NATO training activities and an emphasis on new members' compatibility with established members. The new task is to make the commitment real to the members that joined in 1999—Poland, Hungary, and the Czech Republic. In this sense, U.S. forces need to assist the new members with integration so that 10 to 15 years from now there will be no meaningful difference between these member countries and others (e.g., Greece and Spain) in terms of the quality of their membership in NATO and NATO's ability to defend them. Equally important is to emphasize the new members' compatibility for NATO's more likely missions of conflict management and prevention and peace operations. The success attained in integrating the new members' militaries into NATO will determine the success of enlargement at the political level. At stake is the credibility of

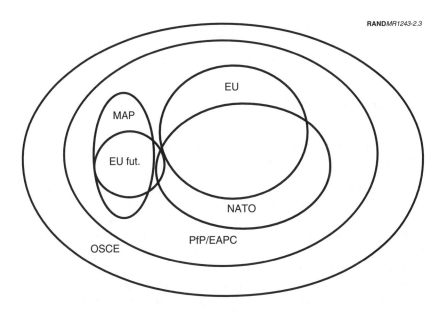

RAND*MR1243-2.3*

Figure 2.3—Overlap Representation of NATO Security Commitment with Respect to European Security Institutions

RAND*MR1243-2.4*

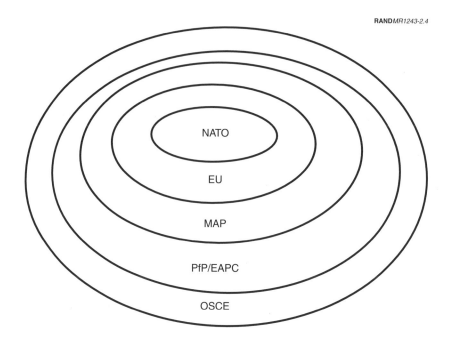

Figure 2.4—Decreasing Levels of NATO Security Commitment

NATO's collective defense commitment and the principle of non-differentiation within NATO.[39]

The second group in Figure 2.4, which is formed by EU members not in NATO—Sweden, Ireland, Finland, and Austria—carries implied NATO security guarantees. Because of the largely coterminous membership of NATO and the EU, a threat to the territory of a non-NATO EU member would involve the major European NATO states through the "back-door" commitment implied by their being members in both organizations. The close integration of EU members, including a deepening common security and foreign policy stance, as well as deepening military cooperation within the EU (over and

---

[39]For an assessment of the potential problems involved in this process, see Daniel N. Nelson and Thomas S. Szayna, "NATO's Metamorphosis and Its New Members," *Problems of Post-Communism*, 45:4, July/August 1998, pp. 32–43.

above the military cooperation within NATO),[40] makes it inconceivable that the major EU members that are also NATO members would not act militarily, if need be, in support of a non-NATO EU member. The responsibilities go beyond NATO membership, as the major NATO and EU members have larger shared economic and political interests in addition to the treaty-specified collective defense responsibilities. How such a commitment might become a NATO matter is the provision for security consultations under Article 4 of the Washington Treaty. But whatever the form that NATO support might take, EU membership carries with it an implicit NATO security guarantee only slightly less credible than an Article 5 commitment. Some of the EU gray-area differences eventually may be erased— Austria, Finland, and Sweden have had internal debates on NATO membership for almost a decade, and given further internal political shifts or evolution of the international security situation, one or more of these three countries might seek NATO membership in the next decade.[41] All of the non-NATO EU countries are PfP members, which allows for substantial military cooperation, whether for NATO support of the country in the case of a threat or, more likely, for NATO-led peace operations. In any event, NATO has a stake in developing military links with the countries in this group, prioritized on the basis of military assets and exposure to hypothetical military threats.

In the third group are PfP countries recognized by NATO to be on the path toward membership—i.e., the MAP countries. There are nine of these: Slovenia, Slovakia, Romania, Macedonia, Lithuania, Latvia, Estonia, Bulgaria, and Albania. The United States and NATO have singled out these states as important to NATO and capable of full integration at some future point, an act that of itself provides a "soft" deterrent to any attempt to intimidate these countries. While there

---

[40]Michael Smith, *Understanding Europe's New Common Foreign and Security Policy*, Institute on Global Conflict and Cooperation, Policy Paper No. 52, March 2000.

[41]For analytical reviews of the debates, see Hanspeter Neuhold, "The Austrian Debate on NATO Membership," in Anton A. Bebler, ed., *The Challenge of NATO Enlargement*, Westport, CT, and London: Praeger, 1999, pp. 188–194; Gunilla Herolf, "The Role of Non-Aligned States in European Defense Organizations: Finland and Sweden," in Mathias Jopp and Hanna Ojanen, eds., *European Security Integration: Implications for Non-Alignment and Alliances*, Programme on the Northern Dimension of the CFSP, Vol. 3, Institute for Security Studies, Western European Union, 1999.

are no guarantees that any of the MAP countries actually will attain membership, the group does represent the set of former communist countries that conceivably might become NATO members in the next 10 to 15 years. By participating in PfP, MAP countries gain access to a mechanism of military cooperation with NATO. Indeed, the premise behind MAP is that the time to begin implementing changes in the militaries of aspiring member states (changes designed to integrate them into NATO) is before, rather than after, accession, which was not the case for the three states that joined in 1999.[42] Most constraints on the extent to which MAP states can cooperate with NATO stem from the MAP states' own (primarily budgetary) problems. NATO has an interest in encouraging continued transition, reform, and cooperative international behavior in these countries, as well as the buildup of military capabilities sufficient to ensure national sovereignty and deterrence and participation in NATO-led peace operations. Some MAP states are likely to join NATO in the not too distant future and/or NATO may be called upon to guarantee their borders even before accession. These are two good reasons to start planning long-term military links with these countries, prioritized on the basis of current and projected military assets, exposure to hypothetical military threat, and strategic importance to NATO.

The fourth group contains the non-MAP European PfP countries: Ukraine, Switzerland, Russia, Moldova, Croatia, and Belarus. Although no countries in this highly diverse group are on track to NATO membership, NATO has an interest in deepening its cooperation with them, especially in peace operations. Because of their large size and their importance to maintaining a benign security environment in Europe, Ukraine and especially Russia stand out in this group, and NATO has established special bilateral relations with both.[43] In the long-term, some countries in this group may emerge

---

[42]This is not to say that far-reaching changes had not taken place in the militaries of the three states that joined in 1999. However, specific steps aimed at integrating the three militaries into NATO did not begin on a full scale until accession was guaranteed. For an analytical review of the considerations behind MAP, see Jeffrey Simon, "Partnership for Peace (PfP): After the Washington Summit and Kosovo," *Strategic Forum*, No. 167, August 1999.

[43]*Founding Act on Mutual Relations, Cooperation and Security Between NATO and the Russian Federation*, May 27, 1997, http://www.nato.int/docu/basictxt/fndact-a.htm; *Charter on a Distinctive Partnership Between the North Atlantic Treaty Organization and Ukraine*, July 9, 1997, http://www.nato.int/docu.basictxt/ukrchrt.htm.

as candidates for NATO membership. Like the MAP countries, these countries have access to a mechanism of military cooperation with NATO by way of PfP. The constraints on the extent of that cooperation vary greatly, from primarily political and self-imposed in the case of Russia and Belarus (and Switzerland), to mainly budgetary in the case of Ukraine and Moldova, and to NATO's own conditions in the case of Croatia. Just as is true for the MAP countries, NATO has a stake in encouraging the former communist states in this group to continue their internal reform processes, to engage in cooperative international behavior, and to participate in NATO-led peace operations (with the last issue also applying to Switzerland). Especially to encourage closer military ties in the future, NATO has an interest in long-term military cooperation with the countries in this group, prioritized on the basis of strategic importance to NATO and military assets.

The final, fifth group in Figure 2.4 comprises the Asian PfP and EAPC countries: Georgia, Azerbaijan, Armenia, Kazakhstan, Kyrgyzstan, Tajikistan, Turkmenistan, and Uzbekistan. This group is of comparatively less interest to NATO, although the countries of south Caucasus (Georgia, Azerbaijan, and Armenia) are more important than the central Asian countries because they border NATO member Turkey. NATO has an interest in supporting the continued sovereignty of all these countries, but even in the long-term, they will remain at best NATO partners in peace operations.[44] Since these countries are members of EAPC, they may appeal to NATO if threatened. So far, however, NATO has shown reluctance to become en-

---

[44]NATO's founding document, the Washington Treaty, contains geographical restrictions on NATO's potential membership. Article 6 specifies membership as limited to European and North American countries, while Article 10 limits the applicability of NATO's membership invitations to European states. Turkey's special status as a country located in both Asia and Europe necessitated special wording to recognize that all of Turkey, not just its European part, is covered by the treaty (Article 6). NATO's stated geographical limits are subject to change, just like any clause in the Washington Treaty, but the strong sense of NATO's organizational identity with Europe (and North America) would make that a lengthy and difficult undertaking. For these reasons, as long as NATO continues to limit its membership to European and North American states, the non-European states will not qualify for membership. In a very different security environment, this situation could change quickly. (U.S. Army wargames in the 2025 time frame have dealt with U.S. forces supporting the defense of Georgia and Turkey, but distant speculation such as this falls outside the scope of this report.)

gaged in the south Caucasus and central Asia in any meaningful form. Nevertheless, NATO does have an interest in encouraging internal reform and democratic development in these countries and in assisting their efforts to build militaries that are compatible and capable of cooperating with NATO.[45]

Two countries fall out of the architecture sketched out above: Bosnia-Herzegovina and FR Yugoslavia (Serbia). Bosnia-Herzegovina, if it emerges as a viable state, may join PfP in the next 10 to 15 years. As for FR Yugoslavia, Serbia's internal evolution will dictate its future extent of cooperation with NATO.

Gray-Area Commitments and Future European Security Trends

The overlapping-areas categorization of NATO's security commitments has important implications for defense planning, especially in relation to possible variations in future European security trends. The priorities outlined above are based on the assumption that the current main security trends in Europe will continue. Looked at using the framework provided by uncertainty-sensitive planning, these trends become the basis for a "no-surprises" future:[46]

- The continued prominence of NATO as the leading security institution and of NATO's involvement in conflict prevention and conflict management.

---

[45]Richard Sokolsky and Tanya Charlick-Paley, *NATO and Caspian Security: A Mission Too Far?* RAND, MR–1074–AF, 1999.

[46]Uncertainty-sensitive planning is a planning tool whose key feature is a distinction between the core "no-surprises" environment, which is based on a continuation of current trends, and changes that may result from two types of uncertainties: "scheduled" (or recognized) uncertainties, and major systemic "shocks" (largely unexpected events that change the entire playing field). Delineation of the uncertainties may lead to the formulation of appropriate strategies: (1) a core strategy for a no-surprises environment; (2) contingent substrategies for dealing with recognized uncertainties; (3) hedging strategies that might deal with shocks; and (4) shaping strategies designed to bring about desirable futures. Uncertainty-sensitive planning is especially appropriate for long-term planning in Europe, since no clear-cut threats are on the horizon but long-term uncertainty about European security still exists. (Paul K. Davis and Zalmay M. Khalilzad, *A Composite Approach to Air Force Planning*, RAND, MR–787–AF, 1996, pp. 17–19.)

- The further deepening of the EU as it takes on increased security functions and succeeds in creating at least the semblance of a "European pillar" in NATO.

- The continued gradual integration of the European former communist states into the political and security framework of NATO and the EU.

Continuation of these three trends in itself is central to the fulfillment of the overall U.S. strategic goals in Europe, which stem from the overarching global U.S. "engagement and enlargement" strategy pursued since the mid-1990s[47] and upheld in every major U.S. strategy statement of the past five years.[48] If the strategy is successful, NATO's collective defense functions will remain an important residual providing cohesion and a sense of purpose to the alliance, but NATO's primary function will be to shape the environment, especially by promoting continued peaceful evolution in the unintegrated area of Europe.

It is entirely plausible that the no-surprises future will come about. However, a number of plausible shifts in emphasis, or branches, in the no-surprises security environment could occur over the next 10 to 15 years. Without fundamentally changing the basic environment, such shifts could alter the direction of trends so that over the longer term, the future might look quite different from the original no-surprises future. Such shifts could take various forms:

- A decrease or an increase in NATO's conflict prevention and conflict management roles, which could cause NATO either to de-emphasize its missions beyond current members' territory and return to its former focus on collective defense functions, or to pursue greater activism and interventionism in non-member states.

- A decrease or an increase in the pace of EU integration, which could lead to a greater EU security identity (and a potentially

---

[47]The White House, *A National Security Strategy of Engagement and Enlargement,* Washington, D.C., GPO, July 1994.

[48]For a recent statement of these goals, see The White House, *A National Security Strategy for a New Century,* December 1999, http://www.pub.whitehouse.gov/uri-res/I2R?urn:pdi://oma.eop.gov.us/2000/1/7/1.text.1.

greater EU role as a mechanism for ensuring security in and around Europe) or to slower development of EU defense capabilities.

- A decrease or an increase in the integration pace of the European former communist countries aspiring to NATO and/or EU membership.

Defense planning must recognize the many ways in which the no-surprises future could change. If some of the recognized uncertainties come about, they could have an exponentially increasing effect on the likelihood and pace of enlargement, leading to a multitude of variations in enlargement paths and the commitments they entail. Moreover, the specific effect on enlargement would be difficult to gauge ahead of time, unless the specific circumstances leading to the branch point's emergence were known. If NATO decided to step up the pace of enlargement, it would likely relax some of the membership criteria outlined in its 1995 enlargement study, which would lead to quick accession of many, if not most, of the nine MAP states. Such an evolution would have to be driven by a sense of threat (either political or military) that currently does not exist and is not now expected to develop. The threat's specific nature would dictate which countries would be first in line to join.

In addition to shifts in emphasis, high-impact but low-probability political shocks could derail any or all of the three main trends of the no-surprises future security environment. Such possibilities include

- NATO's lapse into secondary relevance and importance because of a major divergence of security views between NATO's European and North American members.

- A reversal of EU integration processes because of some major event—for example, an economic depression and the consequent, differing national policies for dealing with its effects.

- The ascendancy to power in several former communist countries of nationalist forces that see the EU and NATO as threats to their sovereignty.

While none of these shocks seems particularly likely to happen, historical experience teaches humility. In 1985, few could have predicted that in the space of 15 years, Europe would witness the unification of the two German states, the mostly peaceful breakup of the USSR, and the entry of Poland, the Czech Republic, and Hungary into NATO. Should a major systemic shock come to pass, it will affect much of the earlier discussion about enlargement.

Implications for Military Planning

To sum up, the process of NATO's enlargement and cooperation with non-members is politically driven in that it seeks to shape the European security environment in conditions involving no specific threat. This process has far-reaching military implications:

- Some of NATO's obligations are straightforward, including the tasks it needs to perform with respect to new members as delineated in the Washington Treaty, and the tasks it may engage in with the fourth (non-MAP European PfP) and fifth (non-European PfP and EAPC) groups in the levels-of-commitment categorization (see Figure 2.4).

- The nature of cooperation and planning with the countries in the third (MAP) group and to a lesser extent the second (non-NATO EU) group is complex, multidimensional, and unclear even though these countries are the ones to which NATO has extended implicit and conditional security guarantees. Even though the pace and extent of military cooperation with these countries are murky, NATO could be called upon to assist these countries in responding to unexpected contingencies in the next 10 to 15 years.

- The situation calls for core strategies designed to ensure that the MAP countries can safeguard their sovereignty (by building a minimum credible deterrent through a combination of NATO assistance measures and making optimal use of scarce defense resources in a NATO context). It also calls for hedging strategies focused primarily on the possible need to assist MAP countries if there is a shift in the no-surprises future.

Through numerous everyday activities, the U.S. armed forces, both continental United States (CONUS) and Europe-based, play a crucial role in implementing the core strategy and shaping the environment so as to advance the no-surprises trends.[49]   They also play an important role in implementing the U.S. hedging strategy—an insurance policy against major shocks—that relies on the continuation of NATO's collective defense functions. To illustrate, seven of EUCOM's eleven strategic objectives pertain to shaping the environment, and three deal directly with NATO's transformation and enlargement: (1) maintain, support, and contribute to the integrity and adaptation of NATO; (2) help prepare the militaries of invited nations to integrate with NATO; and (3) promote stability, democratization, military professionalism, and closer relationships with NATO in the nations of central Europe and the Newly Independent States.[50] United States Air Forces in Europe (USAFE) plays an important role in implementing the U.S. shaping strategy and can assist greatly in advancing U.S. policies toward the new members and MAP states through bilateral training exercises, PfP, staff exchanges, aircrew exchanges, and pilot training in USAFE aircraft. In this context, the pace of enlargement, and the consequent clarification of security guarantees and their attendant obligations, is a major determinant of the type and extent of cooperation between NATO (and specifically the U.S. armed forces) and the MAP states.

The next chapter explores in detail the mechanics of the enlargement process and presents a framework for anticipating how the process may play out for specific MAP countries.

---

[49]The latest (2000) *Annual Report to the President and the Congress* by the Secretary of Defense reemphasizes the shaping role of the armed forces as part of the overall "Shape, Prepare, Respond" national strategy.   For the full report, see http://www.dtic.mil/execsec/adr2000/.

[50]U.S. EUCOM, *Strategy of Readiness and Engagement,* 1998, http://www.eucom.mil/strategy/98strategy.pdf.

Chapter Three

PATTERNS IN THE ENLARGEMENT PROCESS

As envisioned and implemented so far, the enlargement process is long-term and has neither milestones nor deadlines for completion. It is an open process that in principle does not reject beforehand the membership of any European country (as stipulated in Article 10 of the Washington Treaty). Since early 1994, NATO has committed itself to a gradual and transparent process of enlargement, although the meaning of *gradual and transparent* is subject to interpretation. If we assume a no-surprises evolution, forecasts of enlargement in the 2000–10 decade can range from a slow pace of one to two new members to a stepped-up pace of two to three rounds of enlargement, each involving more than one new member. Either of these paths, as well as any number of in-between options, is plausible. But given the driving forces at play and the process's evolution so far, the more likely pathways are in the former, slower category.

The primary reason for a likely slower pace is that the urgency leading up to NATO's enlargement in 1997–99 has dissipated. That initial enlargement was driven by the strong advocacy of the United States and Germany, as well as by a strategic imperative to demonstrate NATO's continued importance in post–Cold War Europe. The 1997–99 enlargement put to rest any doubts about NATO's commitment to taking in new members, and NATO's involvement in peace operations in the Balkans beginning in 1995 demonstrated its continued relevance. Consequently, with the main driving forces no longer so pressing, NATO's enlargement has ceased to be a major topic in discussions of NATO's future. Instead, the agenda is now dominated by discussions of measures to improve the compatibility and interoperability of NATO's armed forces, the implications of long-term NATO involvement in the Balkans, and the extent of potential future NATO involvement in peacemaking. With the first round of enlargement completed and efforts focused on successful integration of the new members, no one questions the genuineness of NATO's enlargement process.

Nonetheless, NATO remains under pressure to continue its enlargement. Too long of a gap between admissions, especially when countries evidently meet NATO's pre-conditions and wish to become members, will lead to doubts about NATO's commitment. Theoretically, such doubts could decrease the strength of the shaping incentives and the behavioral regime that the enlargement process was designed to help bring about in the first place.

The pace of enlargement would change, of course, if the security environment deteriorated rapidly and a military threat arose. Under such circumstances, military, rather than political, imperatives would become the important drivers of the process, possibly leading to quick accession of new members. Absent such a shock, however, the behavioral regime and inducement aspects of enlargement require that the process be slow, deliberate, and transparent.

TIME FRAME OF DECISIONMAKING

A review of the pattern of enlargement followed in 1994–99 is instructive in determining what leeway NATO has in keeping credible its commitment to enlarge under conditions of a continuing benign security environment. If the origins of the enlargement process are dated back to the 1989 fall of the communist regimes in Poland, Czechoslovakia, and Hungary and the 1989–90 NATO decisions to establish cooperative relations with the Warsaw Pact states, then almost 10 years elapsed before Poland, the Czech Republic (the main successor state to Czechoslovakia), and Hungary were admitted to NATO. In comparison, seven years elapsed between the breakdown of authoritarianism in Spain in 1975 and Spain's acceptance into NATO in 1982.

However, a more appropriate starting point for the actual enlargement process is NATO's unveiling of the double track of partnership and potential membership to the former foes in January 1994. With that date as the starting point, five years elapsed before the three new members acceded to NATO in March 1999. This process was punctuated by NATO's formulation of membership criteria for aspiring members in September 1995, its issuing of invitations to the three countries in July 1997, and its ratification of their accession by all existing NATO members, with a U.S. Senate vote in April 1998.[1]

NATO has committed itself to a further enlargement decision in 2002.[2] Any invitees in 2002 might join in 2004, if the ratification and preparation process takes about a year and a half, as it did in the 1997–99 round of enlargement. What emerges is a five-year time span between accessions. Under the current benign security conditions, this span of time seems necessary to build up NATO consensus for a new member, place the issue on NATO's agenda, and ratify the new member's entry. If the same pattern recurs in the future, the third round might start in 2006–07 and lead to accession in 2008–09, and a fourth round might take place in 2012–14. This pattern, if it can be called such, is far from a given, however, and would apply only under no-surprises conditions.

Because the urgency that drove the initial round of enlargement has subsided, future rounds seem more likely to entail single- or double-country rather than multiple-country (three or more) accessions. Furthermore, it is entirely plausible that the 2002 enlargement decision may turn out to be a non-decision in that there may be no consensus or no candidate(s) that clearly meets NATO's pre-conditions, which means no country will be invited.

---

[1]For the major documents pertaining to NATO enlargement, see the annual list of speeches by NATO officials; http://www.nato.int/docu/speech/sp95.htm (through sp98.htm). For a U.S. participant's tracing of the process of NATO enlargement, see Gerald B. Solomon, *The NATO Enlargement Debate, 1990–97: Blessings of Liberty*, Westport, CT, and London: Praeger, 1998. For a review of the way the actual decisionmaking process in the United States evolved with respect to NATO enlargement, see James M. Goldgeier, *Not Whether But When; The U.S. Decision to Enlarge NATO*, Washington, D.C.: Brookings Institution Press, 1999.

[2]NATO has committed itself to review the accession process of the MAP countries at the NATO summit that is to be held "no later than 2002" (Washington Summit Communique issued by the Heads of State and Government participating in the meeting of the North Atlantic Council, Washington, D.C., April 24, 1999, point 7; http://www.nato.int/docu/pr/1999/p99-064e.htm).

Thus, even if the existing security trends continue, the size of enlargement could vary widely. With up to three decisions on enlargement in the next 15 years, NATO could have as many as 22 to 25 members by 2015. Each decision could lead to an invitation to one or more states, though it seems likely that the process will proceed at a slower pace and take in only one or two states per round. Alternatively, and especially if the security environment shows signs of change, several countries might be invited or, conversely, the whole enlargement process might come to a halt. These are all speculations, of course, but they are based on a consideration of the pressures NATO will face to enlarge further, as well as the emerging pattern of the enlargement process.

MECHANICS OF ENLARGEMENT

Because the enlargement process has become regularized, analytically speaking, it can be divided into five distinct stages:

1. Development of military cooperation with the given country under the auspices of Partnership for Peace (PfP).

2. A step-up in PfP cooperation that may include an implicit or explicit formulation of aspiration to membership by the given country and actions within PfP to advance that goal.

3. Consensus-building within NATO regarding the given country's eligibility for consideration for membership, crowned with NATO's open recognition of the aspiration.

4. Detailed scrutiny of the pros and cons of the country's potential accession and discussion of the country's shortcomings in meeting membership pre-conditions.

5. Intra-alliance bargaining as to when the country will be invited to join.

Each of the members that joined in 1997–99 went through this process, and future members are likely to go through a similar process.

Stage 1 is simply an expression of willingness by a given country to cooperate with NATO. This move, which shows a measure of common views toward security and the country's perception of NATO as a useful institution, requires that both NATO and the country's government decide to engage in cooperation with each other. Joining PfP is not difficult, but it is not automatic. Croatia had expressed a desire to join PfP for years but, because of concerns regarding its government's democratic credentials and its regional behavior, was not invited until May 2000. In general, however, NATO has been open in terms of the PfP program. Countries in Europe and the Asian parts of the former USSR that have wanted to join PfP have by and large done so without difficulty. PfP allows a measure of familiarization and identification of problems to further military cooperation. For some countries, the process of cooperation with NATO stops at this stage because of either NATO's or the country's unwillingness to proceed further.

Stage 2 amounts to a step-up in the given country's cooperation within PfP so that PfP may serve as a preparatory path toward membership. This move, which indicates the country's willingness to engage in cooperation and participation in PfP activities that tie it to NATO more intimately, generally entails that the country increase its expenditures on PfP activities and thus requires that its government decide to shift the focus of its activities with NATO. It also means that NATO has made an implicit decision to engage with the given country in a stepped-up fashion. The transition to this stage is not automatic, although in keeping with the intent of PfP, the onus of the decision lies largely with the country. For example, although Switzerland has joined PfP and participated in many PfP activities, its government has not decided to engage in PfP military activities that would indicate Switzerland's intent to become a NATO member. Should the Swiss decide to step up their level of cooperation, NATO would not be likely to object.

Stage 3 represents a tougher hurdle, as it entails an explicit recognition by NATO that the given country's aspirations go beyond close military cooperation and entail eventual membership. The onus of this decision rests with NATO. Whereas in stage 2 the country may formally state its desire to join NATO, in stage 3 it is up to NATO to recognize this intention and then work with the country to achieve it. This decision is important because it entails a future (possibly distant) vision of the country's inclusion in NATO without committing NATO to the country's near- or even mid-term accession. By not rejecting the country's aspirations, NATO implicitly agrees that such aspirations are realistic. MAP, launched in 1999, commits NATO to an extensive program of assistance to translate these aspirations into reality. NATO's initial recognition of a country's aspirations for membership may take the form of a specific mention in a NATO communique or declaration.

The process for placing a country in this category is far from automatic. It entails substantial intra-alliance bargaining that includes an implicit assessment of the strategic implications of recognizing a country's aspirations. Even though a country has engaged in PfP in a substantive fashion, NATO may not recognize it as being considered for membership. This lack of recognition means that NATO sees the country's aspirations as unrealistic and/or not in accordance with its current view of NATO's future geographical scope. For example, except in the cases of Latvia, Lithuania, and Estonia, NATO has refused to consider even putting on the agenda the possibility of NATO membership for countries that have emerged from the former USSR. A case in point is Ukraine. Periodically, high officials in Ukraine have floated the idea of eventual Ukrainian membership in NATO, but NATO has refused to consider this idea (and has refused to recognize similar ideas voiced by senior officials in Azerbaijan and Georgia). Since Ukraine theoretically qualifies for NATO membership under Article 10 of the Washington Treaty, NATO's rationale for refusing stems from the strategic implications such a move would have for NATO's relations with Russia (which has repeatedly warned against Ukraine joining NATO). NATO's unwillingness to accept Ukraine's aspirations effectively leaves Ukraine in stage 2 of the process. Similar strategic considerations led to Finland's holding off on a membership application after having engaged in a quiet dialogue with NATO about membership.

Once a country's aspirations for membership are recognized, stage 4, the tough intra-alliance debate on the country's shortcomings with respect to NATO membership, begins in earnest. The criteria listed in NATO's 1995 enlargement study serve as a template for the consideration of shortcomings. In bilateral and multilateral meetings with representatives from the aspiring country, officials from NATO or its member countries point out the country's shortcomings and work out (through MAP) a mutually agreed-on program and schedule for rectifying them. Depending on the scope and breadth of the shortcomings, stage 4 can range in length from a few years to decades. Moreover, this stage includes much give-and-take, based on the country's willingness and ability to address identified shortfalls. NATO has documented the aspirations and progress of various countries since the Madrid summit in 1997. For example, Romania and Slovenia have been identified consistently as making progress on the membership track, both in the Madrid (1997) and in the Washington (1999) NATO summit communiques. Stage 4 ends when NATO recognizes that the country meets the minimum pre-conditions for membership. This recognition then serves as a transition to the next stage of the process.

Stage 5, the final step, starts with a consensus recognition among NATO members that the aspiring country has met NATO's pre-conditions and is minimally prepared to function within NATO. This determination is political, as there is a substantial gray area for such decisionmaking, and assessments stem at least partly from the strategic and national goals of existing members. Widespread agreement within NATO that a country is minimally prepared for membership does not automatically lead to an invitation being issued. But once there is consensus about a country's preparation, it is politically embarrassing for NATO to turn down an aspirant, because doing so highlights the fact that criteria not mentioned in NATO's 1995 enlargement study (such as concern about relations with Russia) have come into play. The analytically preferable course of action in such a case is to keep the country in stage 4, requesting further preparation. In addition, the decision to issue an invitation involves complex issues of intra-alliance bargaining, not unlike domestic pork barrel politics. In every stage, but particularly in stages 4 and 5, the aspiring country needs to build political support among NATO's members so as to win support for its membership. Once NATO issues an invitation, there is yet another lengthy period, one in which the parliaments of the existing members and the new member must ratify the accession and NATO must prepare to integrate the new member. For all practical intents and purposes, the aspiring member tends to be treated as a member during this time. Its representatives are allowed into most committee meetings and are exposed first-hand to the way NATO functions.

As the five stages illustrate, the enlargement process has an implicit but clear structure and, on the surface, matches the lofty goal of openness to all qualified and interested states as befits NATO's increasing collective security functions. However, in practice the process gives NATO full freedom to decide whether and when to take in new members and to specify and interpret the conditions for membership as fitting with both NATO's continuing role as a collective defense organization and its need for cohesion and trust among NATO members.

The elaborate structure that has developed for the enlargement process is mostly unstated and implicit but is increasingly understood by all. These are the "rules of the game," and after some initial clarifications, all states concerned—including Russia—have understood them. The next chapter identifies where the various aspiring countries stand with respect to NATO membership based on these rules of the game.

Chapter Four

ASSESSING CANDIDATES FOR FUTURE ACCESSION TO NATO

For planning purposes, the time frame for the MAP states' accession to NATO matters greatly. If a country is likely to be a NATO member in the near-term, then shaping activities should be designed with that in mind. For more distant time frames, shaping activities should be designed to ensure that the potential member can provide for its own credible deterrent and, in order to strengthen that deterrent, that the potential member's military development will be compatible with NATO. This rationale is based on the pre-accession criterion regarding a country's military contribution to NATO and on the assumption that a potential member would not be in a position to join NATO in the near term unless it already had armed forces that could provide a minimum deterrent and secure its sovereignty. Thus, for a near-term accession, NATO has a stake in ensuring that the potential member makes a meaningful contribution to both NATO's collective defense and its peace operations. However, for a more distant accession, the country in question may have armed forces that are neither capable of securing its sovereignty nor compatible with NATO. In this case, since NATO provides a "gray-area" commitment to such countries by placing them in MAP, NATO has a stake in ensuring that they have a minimum credible deterrent. Otherwise, NATO could find itself having to intervene early to assist a MAP country in an unexpected crisis.

To ensure that prospective members use their defense resources efficiently and transparently, NATO has a stake in encouraging defense reform in all MAP countries, regardless of whether the country has near-, mid-, or long-term prospects of joining NATO. In addition,

NATO has a stake in ensuring that each MAP country participates in NATO-sponsored peace operations in order to encourage the country's cooperative international behavior, strengthen its thinking in terms of collective security, and transfer military skills and expertise.

This chapter details the distinctions among the MAP countries and uses a specific methodology to discern the likelihood of membership for specific countries. First, the ability to meet NATO's membership pre-conditions is assessed according to military, political, and economic criteria. Second, a series of cost-benefit analyses is performed to assess what is a vaguer but probably more important element of the membership decision—i.e., the strategic rationale for inviting particular countries to join. Third, a combined overall assessment of the likely time frame for membership is provided. For reasons of comparison and completeness, this chapter also evaluates non-NATO states that are members of the EU, because the two groups—MAP and non-NATO EU—make up the "long list" of states that might join NATO in the next 10 to 15 years. The purpose of this detailed look at the likely political decisions concerning NATO's enlargement is to assist those who are planning for the military implications of these decisions (discussed further in Chapters Five and Six).

MEETING NATO'S PRE-CONDITIONS

The nine MAP countries, which are all in stage 3 or 4 of the enlargement process (see Chapter Three for an explanation of these stages), differ from each other in terms of the strategic and political criteria and the time frame for membership likelihood. On the basis of the criteria for categorizing and prioritizing the aspiring countries, the MAP group may be divided into three subgroups. Two countries (Slovakia and Slovenia) form the "early group," five (Bulgaria, Romania, Lithuania, Estonia, and Latvia) form the "middle group," and two (Albania and Macedonia) form the "long-term group." These last two countries are in a different position from the others in that even though NATO has recognized their aspirations by moving them up to stage 3, they remain candidates only in the long run. The countries in the other two subgroups are all in stage 4, so their possibilities for membership are in the mid-term and are currently subject to intra-alliance bargaining. As a visible indication of this differentiation, NATO's 1999 summit communique "recognizes" or "notes and welcomes" the efforts of the early and middle group countries toward NATO membership but only "thanks" Albania and Macedonia for their cooperation.[1]

General Characteristics

A snapshot of population size and GDP can provide an approximation of the differences between aspiring and current NATO members, thus indicating the level of difficulty that NATO and the aspiring members might experience in trying to work within the NATO framework. A combination of high GDP per capita and small population is best for ease of integration, whereas a combination of low GDP per capita and large population is worst. Table 4.1 presents the general characteristics of the nine MAP states. For comparison, Tables 4.2, 4.3, and 4.4 present the same information for EU members not in NATO, other PfP European members, and NATO Europe, respectively.

As a general principle, any new NATO member should be at least comparable to the NATO country having the lowest GDP per capita (currently, Turkey). The greater the per capita GDP, the easier the country is likely to fit into NATO. Of the nine aspirants, only Slovakia and Slovenia (the early group) have GDP per capita figures higher than Turkey's, whether using power purchasing parity (PPP) or exchange rate figures (see Table 4.5). The middle group ranges from Estonia's near parity with Turkey to Romania's much lower figures. Of the long-term group, Macedonia is close to the laggards in the middle group (Romania and Bulgaria).

In terms of population size, Slovenia, Estonia, and Latvia are extremely small (fewer than 2.5 million people), while Lithuania and Slovakia are just small (3.5 to 5.5 million people). Slovenia has no easy counterpart among current NATO members, having less than half the population of Norway but more than four times the population of Luxembourg. Slovakia is close in population size to

---

[1]Washington Summit Communique issued by the Heads of State and Government participating in the meeting of the North Atlantic Council, Washington, D.C., April 24, 1999, point 7, http://www.nato.int/docu/pr/1999/p99-O64e.htm.

Table 4.1

General Characteristics: MAP States

State	Total Population (in 000's)[a]	GDP (PPP, in billions of US$), 1999[b]	GDP Per Capita, 1999 (PPP)[c]	GDP (in billions of US$), 1999[d]	GDP Per Capita, 1999[e]
Albania	3,490	5.6	1,605	3.3[f]	946
Bulgaria	7,797	34.9	4,476	12.1	1,552
Estonia	1,431	7.9	5,521	5.1	3,564
Latvia	2,405	9.8	4,075	6.7	2,786
Lithuania	3,621	17.3	4,778	10.5	2,900
Macedonia	2,041	7.6	3,724	3.4	1,666
Romania	22,411	87.4	3,900	33.8	1,508
Slovakia	5,408	45.9	8,487	19.3	3,569
Slovenia	1,928	21.4	11,100	20.7	10,737

[a]CIA estimates for mid-2000, *The World Factbook 2000*, http://www.odci.gov/cia/publications/factbook/index.html.

[b]CIA figures for 1999, *The World Factbook 2000*, http://www.odci.gov/cia/publications/factbook/index.html.

[c]CIA figures, calculated by dividing the GDP (PPP) figure by total population. Figures here may be slightly different from the per capita figures provided by CIA in *The World Factbook*.

[d]World Bank development data (as of July 2000), at market prices, using current US$. Dollar figures are converted from domestic currencies using single-year official exchange rates (where the official rates reflect effective rates); http://www.worldbank.org/data/countrydata /countrydata.html.

[e]World Bank figures, calculated by dividing the GDP (World Bank exchange rate data) by total population.

[f]Estimated.

Table 4.2

General Characteristics: Non-NATO EU Members

State	Total Population (in 000's)[a]	GDP (PPP, in billions of US$), 1999[b]	GDP Per Capita, 1999 (PPP)[c]	GDP (in billions of US$), 1999[d]	GDP Per Capita, 1999[e]
Austria	8,131	190.6	23,441	208.9	25,692
Finland	5,167	108.6	21,018	126.1	24,405
Ireland	3,797	73.7	19,410	84.9	22,360
Sweden	8,873	184.0	20,737	226.4	25,516

[a]CIA estimates for mid-2000, *The World Factbook 2000*, http://www.odci.gov/cia/ publications/factbook/index.html.

[b]CIA figures for 1999, *The World Factbook 2000*, http://www.odci.gov/cia/publications/factbook/index.html.

[c]CIA figures, calculated by dividing the GDP (PPP) figure by total population. Figures here may be slightly different from the per capita figures provided by CIA in *The World Factbook*.

[d]World Bank development data (as of July 2000), at market prices, using current US$. Dollar figures are converted from domestic currencies using single-year official exchange rates (where the official rates reflect effective rates); http://www.worldbank.org/data/countrydata/countrydata.html.

[e]World Bank figures, calculated by dividing the GDP (World Bank exchange rate data) by total population.

Table 4.3

General Characteristics: Other European PfP Members
(Non-EU, Non-MAP)

State	Total Population (in 000's)[a]	GDP (PPP, in billions of US$), 1999[b]	GDP per Capita, 1999 (PPP)[c]	GDP (in billions of US$), 1999[d]	GDP per Capita, 1999[e]
Belarus	10,367	55.2	5,325	27.2[f]	2,624
Croatia	4,282	23.9	5,582	21.3[f]	4,974
Moldova	4,431	9.7	2,189	1.1	248
Russia	146,002	620.3	4,249	375.3	2,571
Switzerland	7,262	197.0	27,128	260.3	35,844
Ukraine	49,153	109.5	2,228	37.3[f]	759

[a]CIA estimates for mid-2000, *The World Factbook 2000*, http://www.odci.gov/cia/publications/factbook/index.html.
[b]CIA figures for 1999, *The World Factbook 2000*, http://www.odci.gov/cia/publications/factbook/index.html.
[c]CIA figures, calculated by dividing the GDP (PPP) figure by total population. Figures here may be slightly different from the per capita figures provided by CIA in *The World Factbook*.
[d]World Bank development data (as of July 2000), at market prices, using current US$. Dollar figures are converted from domestic currencies using single-year official exchange rates (where the official rates reflect effective rates); http://www.worldbank.org/data/countrydata/countrydata.html.
[e]World Bank figures, calculated by dividing the GDP (World Bank exchange rate data) by total population.
[f]Estimated.

Denmark. Romania, with its large population size, also has no easy counterparts in NATO; its population is larger than that of Netherlands but much smaller than that of Poland. Bulgaria's population is close to that of Portugal. Of the four non-NATO EU members, all have GDP per capita rates that exceed or fall near the median of current NATO Europe members. All have small populations, with even the largest (Sweden) having fewer people than Portugal.

Defense Expenditures

In terms of a country's ability to contribute militarily to NATO, the more important indicators involve defense expenditures and size of armed forces. A snapshot of defense expenditures, expressed as a percentage of GDP and in per capita terms, presents a general picture of a country's defense burden. Defense expenditures fluctuate

Table 4.4

General Characteristics: NATO Europe

State	Total Population (in 000's)[a]	GDP (PPP, in billions of US$), 1999[b]	GDP Per Capita, 1999 (PPP)[c]	GDP (in billions of US$), 1999[d]	GDP Per Capita, 1999[e]
Belgium	10,242	243.4	23,765	245.7	23,989
Czech Rep.	10,272	120.8	11,760	56.3[f]	5,481
Denmark	5,336	127.7	23,932	174.4	32,684
France	59,330	1,373.0	23,142	1,400.0	23,597
Germany	82,797	1,864.0	22,513	2,100.0	25,363
Greece	10,602	149.2	14,073	123.9	11,686
Hungary	10,139	79.4	7,831	48.4	4,774
Iceland	276	6.4	23,188	8.5	30,797
Italy	57,634	1,212.0	21,029	1,100.0	19,086
Luxembourg	437	14.7	33,638	17.6	40,275
Netherlands	15,892	365.1	22,974	384.8	24,213
Norway	4,481	111.3	24,838	145.4	32,448
Poland	38,646	276.5	7,155	154.1	3,987
Portugal	10,048	151.4	15,068	107.7	10,719
Spain	39,997	677.5	16,939	562.2	14,056
Turkey	65,667	409.4	6,234	188.4	2,869
United Kingdom	59,511	1,290.0	21,677	1,400.0	23,525

[a]CIA estimates for mid-2000, *The World Factbook 2000*, http://www.odci.gov/cia/publications/factbook/index.html.
[b]CIA figures for 1999, *The World Factbook 2000*, http://www.odci.gov/cia/publications/factbook/index.html.
[c]CIA figures, calculated by dividing the GDP (PPP) figure by total population. Figures here may be slightly different from the per capita figures provided by CIA in *The World Factbook*.
[d]World Bank development data (as of July 2000), at market prices, using current US$. Dollar figures are converted from domestic currencies using single-year official exchange rates (where the official rates reflect effective rates); http://www.worldbank.org/data/countrydata/countrydata.html.
[e]World Bank figures, calculated by dividing the GDP (World Bank exchange rate data) by total population.
[f]Estimated.

Table 4.5

GDP Per Capita Comparison: MAP States and Current NATO "Floor"

State	GDP per Capita, 1999 (PPP)[a]	GDP Per Capita, 1999 (PPP), as % of NATO "Floor"[b]	GDP Per Capita, 1999 (XR)[a]	GDP (Per Capita, 1999 (XR), as % of NATO "Floor"[c]	Overall Score[d]
Albania	1,605	25.7	946	33.0	Low (29.4)
Bulgaria	4,476	71.8	1,552	54.1	Medium-low (63.0)
Estonia	5,521	88.6	3,564	124.2	High (106.4)
Latvia	4,075	65.4	2,786	97.1	Medium-high (81.3)
Lithuania	4,778	76.6	2,900	101.1	Medium-high (88.9)
Macedonia	3,724	59.7	1,666	58.1	Medium-low (58.9)
Romania	3,900	62.6	1,508	52.6	Medium-low (57.6)
Slovakia	8,487	136.1	3,569	124.4	High (130.1)
Slovenia	11,100	178.1	10,737	374.2	High (276.2)

[a]Data from Table 4.1.
[b]The current NATO "floor" is Turkey, at $6,234 (Table 4.4).
[c]The current NATO "floor" is Turkey, at $2,869 (Table 4.4).
[d]Overall score is a median of the percentages from columns 3 and 5 (GDP per capita, expressed in PPP and exchange rate [XR]). Each score was assigned one of four assessments: high, medium-high, medium-low, and low. High was a score above the "floor" level; medium-high was a score ranging from 67 to 100 percent of the "floor" level; medium-low was a score ranging from 33 to 66 percent of the "floor" level; low was a score below 32 percent of the "floor" level.

from year to year, but in the current conditions of a benign security environment, they seldom change by more than 0.2 percent of GDP per year. Thus, the snapshot presents an approximation of the current defense burden in a comparative fashion. Median defense expenditures (expressed as a percentage of GDP) have declined to 2.0 percent in NATO Europe. Aspiring NATO members will need to keep their defense spending at approximately that level to be seen as making serious efforts to contribute to NATO. Indeed, NATO has made the 2-percent-of-GDP threshold a goal for aspiring members, and this goal is explicit in the specific membership action plans already agreed to. In any event, a country spending at levels less than 25 percent below the median (1.5 percent of GDP) would be suspected of being a prospective free rider and thus not suitable for membership candidacy. Since less-affluent countries may carry a heavy defense burden but still not spend all that much on defense in absolute terms, the calculation of defense spending on a per capita (population) basis provides a complementary measure to the defense burden expressed as a percentage of GDP. Having both a defense burden near or above the NATO Europe median and a high (over $400) defense expenditure per capita is the best situation for ease of integration, whereas having low figures in both categories is the worst.

Defense expenditures per troop provide a rough measure of the technological sophistication of a country's armed forces. The technologically most advanced armed forces in the world spend well over 100,000 US$ per troop, although the current NATO Europe median is at $93,607 (Italy). A combination of a defense burden near the NATO Europe median and a high per-troop spending ratio would be best for ease of integration into NATO. A low level of defense expenditures as a percentage of GDP raises questions about how seriously an aspiring member treats its armed forces and introduces the notion that the country is likely to depend on NATO members for its own security while contributing little to NATO operations. A low level of defense expenditures per troop points to incompatibilities with most current NATO members in that it suggests either too large a force size (and perhaps reform measures that have not gone far enough in cutting back active forces) or, when combined with low defense expenditures as a percentage of GDP, inadequate attention to defense by the country's political leadership. Either way, the lower the technological sophistication of its armed forces, the more difficulty a country will have, in general terms, adjusting to the way NATO approaches combat operations. Table 4.6 presents the defense expenditures of the nine MAP states. For comparison, Tables 4.7, 4.8, and 4.9 present the same information for non-NATO EU members, other PfP European members, and NATO Europe, respectively.

Of the nine MAP states, Macedonia, Bulgaria, Slovakia, and Romania are at or above the NATO median for defense expenditures as a percentage of GDP. Slovenia is lower, at 1.5 percent, the cutoff level for a potential free rider. In terms of defense expenditures per troop, Slovenia is far in the lead, spending at higher levels than four NATO members and approximating Greek spending levels. The rest of the aspirants fall below the NATO country currently having the lowest defense expenditures per troop (Poland, at $14,469).[2] Estonia is at 82 percent of the Polish level, Lithuania is at 67 percent, Slovakia and Latvia are at 63 percent, and the others are lower. A slightly different pattern comes up when comparing defense expenditures per capita. Slovenia is ahead of several current NATO members, but next in line is Slovakia, just slightly behind the current member having the lowest expenditures per capita (Hungary, at $71).[3]

Table 4.6

Defense Expenditures: MAP States

State	Defense Expenditures (in millions of US$), 1999[a]	Defense Expenditures as % of GDP, 1998[b]	Peacetime Active Force Size, 2000[c]	Defense Expenditures/ Troop (in US$), 1999–2000[d]	Defense Expenditures Per Capita (in US$), 1999–2000[e]
Albania	32	1.1	47,000	681	9
Bulgaria	285	2.5	79,760	3,573	37
Estonia	57	1.2	4,800	11,875	40
Latvia	46	0.7	5,050	9,109	19
Lithuania	124	1.3	12,700	9,764	34
Macedonia	117	2.4	16,000	7,313	57
Romania	541	2.2	207,000	2,614	24
Slovakia	352	2.0	38,600	9,119	65
Slovenia	345	1.5	9,000	38,333	179

[a]Calculated by SIPRI; data are in constant US$ (based on constant 1995 prices and exchange rates), *SIPRI Yearbook, 2000.*

[b]Calculated by SIPRI for latest year available (1998), *SIPRI Yearbook, 2000.*

[c]From IISS (International Institute for Strategic Studies), *The Military Balance, 2000–2001.*

[d]Calculated by dividing defense expenditures (column 2) by peacetime active force size (column 4).

[e]Calculated by dividing defense expenditures (column 2) by total population (CIA estimates, in Table 4.1).

---

[2]Iceland is not considered in these calculations, since it does not have armed forces.

[3]For the same reason explained in the preceding footnote, Iceland is not considered here, either.

Table 4.7

Defense Expenditures: Non-NATO EU Members

State	Defense Expenditures (in millions of US$), 1999[a]	Defense Expenditures as % of GDP, 1998[b]	Peacetime Active Force Size, 2000[c]	Defense Expenditures/ Troop (in US$), 1999–2000[d]	Defense Expenditures Per Capita (in US$), 1999–2000[e]
Austria	2,131	0.8	35,500	60,028	262
Finland	1,913	1.5	31,700	60,347	370
Ireland	871	0.8	11,460	76,003	229
Sweden	5,714	2.2	52,700	108,425	644

[a]Calculated by SIPRI; data are in constant US$ (based on constant 1995 prices and exchange rates), *SIPRI Yearbook, 2000.*

[b]Calculated by SIPRI for latest year available (1998), *SIPRI Yearbook, 2000.*

[c]From IISS, *The Military Balance, 2000–2001.*

[d]Calculated by dividing defense expenditures (column 2) by peacetime active force size (column 4).

[e]Calculated by dividing defense expenditures (column 2) by total population (CIA estimates, in Table 4.2).

Table 4.8

Defense Expenditures: Other European PfP Members (Non-EU, Non-MAP)

State	Defense Expenditures (in millions of US$), 1999[a]	Defense Expenditures as % of GDP, 1998[b]	Peacetime Active Force Size, 2000[c]	Defense Expenditures/ Troop (in US$), 1999–2000[d]	Defense Expenditures Per Capita (in US$), 1999–2000[e]
Belarus	400	1.0	83,100	4,813	39
Croatia	926	6.2	61,000	15,180	216
Moldova	15	0.6	9,500	1,579	3
Russia	22,400	3.2	1,004,100	22,308	153
Switzerland	3,718	1.2	27,970	132,928	512
Ukraine	1,380	3.6	303,800	4,542	28

[a]Calculated by SIPRI; data are in constant US$ (based on constant 1995 prices and exchange rates), *SIPRI Yearbook, 2000.*

[b]Calculated by SIPRI for latest year available (1998), *SIPRI Yearbook, 2000.*

[c]From IISS, *The Military Balance, 2000–2001.*

[d]Calculated by dividing defense expenditures (column 2) by peacetime active force size (column 4).

[e]Calculated by dividing defense expenditures (column 2) by total population (CIA estimates, in Table 4.3).

Table 4.9

Defense Expenditures: NATO Europe

State	Defense Expenditures (in millions of US$), 1999[a]	Defense Expenditures as % of GDP, 1998[b]	Peacetime Active Force Size, 2000[c]	Defense Expenditures/ Troop (in US$), 1999–2000[d]	Defense Expenditures Per Capita (in US$), 1999–2000[e]
Belgium	4,386	1.5	39,250	111,745	428
Czech Rep.	1,175	2.1	57,700	20,364	114
Denmark	3,223	1.6	21,810	147,776	604
France	46,792	2.8	294,430	158,924	789
Germany	39,543	1.5	321,000	123,187	478
Greece	6,543	4.8	159,170	41,107	617
Hungary	715	1.3	43,790	16,328	71
Iceland	0	0	0	0	0
Italy	23,458	2.0	250,600	93,607	407
Luxembourg	177	0.8	899	196,885	405
Netherlands	7,851	1.8	51,940	151,155	494
Norway	3,650	2.3	26,700	136,704	815
Poland	3,144	2.1	217,290	14,469	81
Portugal	2,685	2.2	44,650	60,134	267
Spain	8,675	1.4	166,050	52,243	217
Turkey	9,588	4.4	609,700	15,725	146
UK	31,810	2.7	212,450	149,729	535

[a]Calculated by SIPRI; data are in constant US$ (based on constant 1995 prices and exchange rates), *SIPRI Yearbook, 2000.*
[b]Calculated by SIPRI for latest year available (1998), *SIPRI Yearbook, 2000.*
[c]From IISS, *The Military Balance, 2000–2001.*
[d]Calculated by dividing defense expenditures (column 2) by peacetime active force size (column 4).
[e]Calculated by dividing defense expenditures (column 2) by total population (CIA estimates, in Table 4.4).

Of the non-NATO EU members, Sweden spends more on defense (as a percentage of GDP) than the median in NATO Europe, Finland spends at the 1.5 percent (free-rider cutoff) level, and Austria does not spend enough to be considered as a potential contributing member to NATO. A similar pattern emerges when comparing defense expenditures per capita. In terms of defense expenditures per troop, Sweden again ranks high with NATO Europe countries (above the NATO Europe median), while Finland and Austria spend at levels below the NATO Europe median (close to the level of Portugal).[4]

It is important that pre-condition thresholds and goals for new members not be set at unrealistically high levels. An aspiring country's ability to meet the pre-conditions says nothing about the strategic wisdom of inviting that country to join NATO, but if the country matches or exceeds the current NATO "floor" (as represented by the NATO country having the lowest figures in a given category) in terms of how it treats its armed forces and defense, then it can be said to have attained minimum NATO standards. In this sense, when they joined NATO, Poland, the Czech Republic, and arguably Hungary (by most measures) met or exceeded the minimum NATO standards for GDP per capita, defense expenditures as a percentage of GDP, and defense expenditures per troop.[5] In the current list of nine aspirants, Slovenia and Slovakia either exceed or are close to these standards, though some doubts may remain about Slovenia's low defense expenditures as a percentage of GDP (its low defense burden) and Slovakia's low defense expenditures per troop. None of the other aspiring members is currently close to meeting the minimum NATO standards. Some (Estonia, Latvia, and Lithuania) come close to the minimum levels in one category but fall well short in the others. Of the non-NATO EU members, Sweden and, with some questions about its defense burden, Finland would not have many problems fitting into NATO. Austria's defense burden is well below the free-rider cutoff level.

The snapshot figures present a general picture but are not particularly informative when it comes to future trends. The best indication

---

[4]Ireland is not considered here any further. There is no serious debate in that country about joining NATO, nor is there any reason to expect such a debate to start in the near future

[5]In 1999, when the three countries became members, Turkey represented the NATO "floor" in GDP per capita (PPP): $6,485. The 1999 Czech, Hungarian, and Polish levels in this category were $11,351, $7,402, and $6,812, respectively. In terms of defense expenditures as a percentage of GDP, Poland was above the NATO median (at 2.3 percent), the Czech Republic was slightly below it (at 1.8 percent), and Hungary fell below the free-rider cutoff level (with a defense burden of 1.1 percent). In terms of defense expenditures per troop, Turkey represented the NATO "floor" in 1999, at $12,394. The 1999 Czech, Hungarian, and Polish levels in this category were $18,230, $13,352, and $12,686, respectively.

of a defense budget's potential future growth is the rate of GDP growth. If the state has sufficient extractive capacity, GDP growth generally allows for growth in state expenditures. Thus, sustained high GDP growth points to the potential for increased expenditures on defense. Table 4.10 presents trends and projections in GDP growth for 1989 through 2003 for the nine aspirants.

Of the early- and middle-group MAP countries, only Slovakia and Slovenia have had a net positive GDP growth over the past decade. Both have had sustained high GDP growth rates (3 to 4 percent per year) for most of the period since 1993–94, and this trend is projected to continue. Estonia, Latvia, and Lithuania suffered enormous contraction in GDP in 1991–93 as a consequence of the Soviet breakup. All three (and especially Estonia) nevertheless have shown high GDP growth rates (4 to 6 percent per year) for most of the period since 1995–96, and although they all were affected negatively by Russia's economic problems in 1998–99, they are expected to grow at 4 to 5 percent per year for the next few years. Bulgaria and Romania exhibit less favorable trends. Reforms in Bulgaria finally led to GDP growth in 1998, and the country is projected to grow at a fast pace in the next few years. After a period of growth in GDP in 1993–96, Romania experienced negative growth in 1997–99, and its economic outlook remains uncertain. As for the long-term group of MAP countries, they have experienced growth in GDP over the past few years, and that trend is expected to continue. Thus, except in the case of Romania, the trends and estimates point to the feasibility of gradual increases in defense expenditures for all aspiring members.

Table 4.10

Trends in GDP Growth: MAP States, 1989–2003

State	1989–99	1995	1996	1997	1998	1999	1999–2003[a]
Albania	1.3	8.9	9.1	−7.0	8.0	7.3	7.7
Bulgaria	−3.3	2.9	−10.1	−7.0	3.5	2.4	4.9
Estonia	−2.5	4.3	3.9	10.6	4.7	−1.1	3.9
Latvia	−3.8	−0.8	3.3	8.6	3.9	0.1	4.6
Lithuania	−4.0	3.3	4.7	7.3	5.1	−4.1	4.3
Macedonia	−0.8	9.1	2.1	1.5	2.9	2.7	5.3
Romania	−1.5	7.1	3.9	−6.6	−4.9	−3.2	N/A
Slovakia	0.9	6.9	6.6	6.5	4.4	1.9	3.9
Slovenia	2.3	4.1	3.5	4.6	3.9	3.8	N/A

SOURCE: World Bank development data, http://www.worldbank.org/data/countrydata/countrydata.html; World Bank country data profile and country at a glance, http://www.worldbank.org/html/extdr/regions.htm.
[a]World Bank projected average annual growth rate of GDP.

Political and Economic Criteria

In line with the enlargement process goal of establishing incentives for reform in the transitioning countries, new members need to show that they have fully established democratic political institutions and market economies. Whereas the indicators discussed above concentrate on a country's ability and willingness to contribute militarily to NATO at a reasonable level, three of the five pre-conditions concern democratic governance. Freedom House is one of the best known and most credible institutions that gauge the political and civil rights of all countries in the world according to a standard methodology. Table 4.11 shows annual Freedom House ratings since 1990 for each of the MAP states. For comparison, Tables 4.12, 4.13, and 4.14 present the same information for non-NATO EU members, other PfP European members, and NATO Europe, respectively.

With the exception of Turkey, which receives a partly free (PF) rating, and some questions regarding the extent of civil liberties in Greece, all current NATO Europe countries have a free (F) rating and scores of 1+1 or 1+2 (political + civil rights) on the Freedom House scale. With that score as a pre-condition threshold for aspiring members, Slovenia, Slovakia, Lithuania, Estonia, and Latvia already qualify, with Slovenia's record of political and civil rights since 1993–94 being indistinguishable from that of most NATO Europe countries. Romania, with a 2+2 rating, is almost at the level of most NATO Europe countries, followed by Bulgaria (2+3). Albania and Macedonia receive a partly free rating. Thus, based on the Freedom House assessment of their democratization process in the 1990s, the early and middle groups of NATO aspirants are either at or near the ratings received by most NATO countries. The three NATO members that joined in 1999 had all achieved a 1+2 rating between 1993 and 1995. The non-NATO EU members have 1+1 ratings. The former Soviet states that participate in PfP are all rated partly free except for Belarus, which is rated not free.

More detailed assessments of the aspiring countries' progress in the transition process show a similar but more nuanced picture. Other than Albania and Macedonia, all NATO aspirants, as well as the three NATO members that joined in 1999, are on track to EU membership.

Table 4.11

Freedom House Ratings: MAP States, 1991–2000

State	1991– 1992	1992– 1993	1993– 1994	1994– 1995	1995– 1996	1996– 1997	1997– 1998	1998– 1999	1999– 2000
Albania	4,4,PF	4,3,PF	2,4,PF	3,4,PF	3,4,PF	4,4,PF	4,4,PF	4,5,PF	4,5,PF
Bulgaria	2,3,F	2,3,F	2,2,F	2,2,F	2,2,F	2,3,F	2,3,F	2,3,F	2,3,F
Estonia	2,3,F	3,3,PF	3,2,F	3,2,F	2,2,F	1,2,F	1,2,F	1,2,F	1,2,F
Latvia	2,3,F	3,3,PF	3,3,PF	3,2,F	2,2,F	2,2,F	1,2,F	1,2,F	1,2,F
Lithuania	2,3,F	2,3,F	1,3,F	1,3,F	1,2,F	1,2,F	1,2,F	1,2,F	1,2,F
Macedonia		3,4,PF	3,3,PF	4,3,PF	4,3,PF	4,3,PF	4,3,PF	3,3,PF	3,3,PF
Romania	5,5,PF	4,4,PF	4,4,PF	4,3,PF	4,3,PF	2,3,F	2,2,F	2,2,F	2,2,F
Slovakia		3,4,PF	2,3,F	2,3,F	2,4,PF	2,4,PF	2,2,F	1,2,F
Slovenia	2,3,F	2,2,F	1,2,F	1,2,F	1,2,F	1,2,F	1,2,F	1,2,F	1,2,F

SOURCE: Freedom House. For full explanation of methodology, see http://www.freedomhouse.org/ratings/.

NOTE: In each column, the first number is the political rights index and the second number is the civil liberties index. Both are based on a scale of 1 to 7, with 1 representing the highest degree of freedom and 7 representing the lowest. The third component is a combined assessment of freedom status, represented as F (free), PF (partly free), and NF (not free). If a country's combined averages for political rights and civil liberties fall between 1.0 and 2.5, it is considered free; between 3.0 and 5.5, partly free; and between 5.5 and 7.0, not free.

Table 4.12

Freedom House Ratings: Non-NATO EU Members, 1991–2000

State	1991– 1992	1992– 1993	1993– 1994	1994– 1995	1995– 1996	1996– 1997	1997– 1998	1998– 1999	1999– 2000
Austria	1,1,F	1,1,F	1,1,F	1,1,F	1,1,F	1,1,F	1,1,F	1,1,F	1,1,F
Finland	1,1,F	1,1,F	1,1,F	1,1,F	1,1,F	1,1,F	1,1,F	1,1,F	1,1,F
Ireland	1,1,F	1,1,F	1,2,F	1,2,F	1,1,F	1,1,F	1,1,F	1,1,F	1,1,F
Sweden	1,1,F	1,1,F	1,1,F	1,1,F	1,1,F	1,1,F	1,1,F	1,1,F	1,1,F

SOURCE: Freedom House. For full explanation of methodology, see http://www.freedomhouse.org/ratings/.

NOTE: In each column, the first number is the political rights index and the second number is the civil liberties index. Both are based on a scale of 1 to 7, with 1 representing the highest degree of freedom and 7 representing the lowest. The third component is a combined assessment of freedom status, represented as F (free), PF (partly free), and NF (not free). If a country's combined averages for political rights and civil liberties fall between 1.0 and 2.5, it is considered free; between 3.0 and 5.5, partly free; and between 5.5 and 7.0, not free.

Table 4.13

Freedom House Ratings: Other European PfP Members (Non-EU, Non-MAP), 1991–2000

State	1991–1992	1992–1993	1993–1994	1994–1995	1995–1996	1996–1997	1997–1998	1998–1999	1999–2000
Belarus	4,4,PF	4,3,PF	5,4,PF	4,4,PF	5,5,PF	6,6,NF	6,6,NF	6,6,NF	6,6,NF
Croatia	3,4,PF	4,4,PF	4,4,PF	4,4,PF	4,4,PF	4,4,PF	4,4,PF	4,4,PF	4,4,PF
Moldova	5,4,PF	5,5,PF	5,5,PF	4,4,PF	4,4,PF	3,4,PF	3,4,PF	2,4,PF	2,4,PF
Russia	3,3,PF	3,4,PF	3,4,PF	3,4,PF	3,4,PF	3,4,PF	3,4,PF	4,4,PF	4,5,PF
Switzerland	1,1,F	1,1,F	1,1,F	1,1,F	1,1,F	1,1,F	1,1,F	1,1,F	1,1,F
Ukraine	3,3,PF	3,3,PF	4,4,PF	3,4,PF	3,4,PF	3,4,PF	3,4,PF	3,4,PF	3,4,PF

SOURCE: Freedom House. For full explanation of methodology, see http://www.freedomhouse.org/ratings/.

NOTE: In each column, the first number is the political rights index and the second number is the civil liberties index. Both are based on a scale of 1 to 7, with 1 representing the highest degree of freedom and 7 representing the lowest. The third component is a combined assessment of freedom status, represented as F (free), PF (partly free), and NF (not free). If a country's combined averages for political rights and civil liberties fall between 1.0 and 2.5, it is considered free; between 3.0 and 5.5, partly free; and between 5.5 and 7.0, not free.

Table 4.14

Freedom House Ratings: NATO Europe, 1991–2000

State	1991–1992	1992–1993	1993–1994	1994–1995	1995–1996	1996–1997	1997–1998	1998–1999	1999–2000
Belgium	1,1,F	1,1,F	1,1,F	1,1,F	1,1,F	1,2,F	1,2,F	1,2,F	1,2,F
Czech Rep.			1,2,F	1,2,F	1,2,F	1,2,F	1,2,F	1,2,F	1,2,F
Denmark	1,1,F	1,1,F	1,1,F	1,1,F	1,1,F	1,1,F	1,1,F	1,1,F	1,1,F
France	1,2,F	1,2,F	1,2,F	1,2,F	1,2,F	1,2,F	1,2,F	1,2,F	1,2,F
Germany	1,2,F	1,2,F	1,2,F	1,2,F	1,2,F	1,2,F	1,2,F	1,2,F	1,2,F
Greece	1,2,F	1,2,F	1,3,F	1,3,F	1,3,F	1,3,F	1,3,F	1,3,F	1,3,F
Hungary	2,2,F	2,2,F	1,2,F	1,2,F	1,2,F	1,2,F	1,2,F	1,2,F	1,2,F
Iceland	1,1,F	1,1,F	1,1,F	1,1,F	1,1,F	1,1,F	1,1,F	1,1,F	1,1,F
Italy	1,1,F	1,2,F	1,3,F	1,2,F	1,2,F	1,2,F	1,2,F	1,2,F	1,2,F
Luxembourg	1,1,F	1,1,F	1,1,F	1,1,F	1,1,F	1,1,F	1,1,F	1,1,F	1,1,F
Netherlands	1,1,F	1,1,F	1,1,F	1,1,F	1,1,F	1,1,F	1,1,F	1,1,F	1,1,F
Norway	1,1,F	1,1,F	1,1,F	1,1,F	1,1,F	1,1,F	1,1,F	1,1,F	1,1,F
Poland	2,2,F	2,2,F	2,2,F	2,2,F	1,2,F	1,2,F	1,2,F	1,2,F	1,2,F
Portugal	1,1,F	1,1,F	1,1,F	1,1,F	1,1,F	1,1,F	1,1,F	1,1,F	1,1,F
Spain	1,1,F	1,1,F	1,2,F	1,2,F	1,2,F	1,2,F	1,2,F	1,2,F	1,2,F
Turkey	2,4,PF	2,4,PF	4,4,PF	5,5,PF	5,5,PF	4,5,PF	4,5,PF	4,5,PF	4,5,PF
UK	1,2,F	1,2,F	1,2,F	1,2,F	1,2,F	1,2,F	1,2,F	1,2,F	1,2,F

SOURCE: Freedom House. For full explanation of methodology, see http://www.freedomhouse.org/ratings/.

NOTE: In each column, the first number is the political rights index and the second number is the civil liberties index. Both are based on a scale of 1 to 7, with 1 representing the highest degree of freedom and 7 representing the lowest. The third component is a combined assessment of freedom status, represented as F (free), PF (partly free), and NF (not free). If a country's combined averages for political rights and civil liberties fall between 1.0 and 2.5, it is considered free; between 3.0 and 5.5, partly free; and between 5.5 and 7.0, not free.

In 1997, the EU invited Poland, the Czech Republic, Hungary, Estonia, and Slovenia (as well as Cyprus) to begin accession negotiations. In 1999, the EU did the same for Latvia, Lithuania, Bulgaria, Slovakia, and Romania. Some of the countries in the first group of EU invitees may join the EU as early as 2003–05. The EU has established criteria for political rights associated with democratic governance (similar to NATO's pre-conditions) that prospective EU members will have to meet. Called the Copenhagen criteria, these conditions boil down to "stability of institutions guaranteeing democracy, the rule of law, human rights and respect for one's protection of minorities." In addition, the EU has set up extensive criteria for assessing the extent to which the transitioning countries have transformed their economies to market-based. The EU provides a detailed annual assessment of progress in both areas, political and economic.[6]

The EU assessments are directly relevant to assessments of the NATO aspirants' progress in meeting NATO pre-conditions, especially given how similar the two organizations' criteria are. Since most countries in the EU are also in NATO, there is no reason to believe that EU and NATO evaluations of a country's political and economic progress will differ. Moreover, since accession of new members to the EU raises politically touchy pocketbook issues in all the current EU countries, there are good reasons for the EU to be blunt in its assessments. For all these reasons, the EU assessments provide a useful evaluation of where NATO aspirants stand in meeting most of the NATO pre-conditions. Table 4.15 presents the EU assessments of the nine NATO aspirants from the latest (November 2000) round of EU evaluations.

The EU assessments provide greater differentiation in measuring countries' progress toward consolidation of democratic institutions and market economies. For the aspiring NATO members, four distinguishable gradations in progress in the political realm are evident in the EU evaluations:

---

[6]For an analytical overview of the way the EU is approaching enlargement eastward, see Karen Henderson, "The Challenges of EU Eastward Enlargement," *International Politics*, 37:1, March 2000, pp. 1–17. For key documents and progress reports of EU enlargement, see http://europa.eu.int/comm/enlargement.

Table 4.15

EU Assessment of EU Membership Readiness: MAP States

State	EU Political Criteria Assessment (2000)	EU Economic Criteria Assessment (2000)
Albania	Not on membership track; EU assisting in establishing "democracy and a rule of law"	Not on membership track; EU assisting in transformation "toward a market economy"
Bulgaria	"Continues to fulfill the Copenhagen criteria"; further actions required regarding short-term priorities for accession; problems: weak judicial system, very serious corruption problem, protection of minorities (Roma)	"Has clearly made further progress towards becoming a functioning market economy....not yet able to cope...within the EU in the medium term"
Estonia	"Continues to fulfill the Copenhagen criteria", addressed most short-term priorities for accession, working on medium-term priorities; problems: administrative and judicial reform, integration of minorities and non-citizens	"Is a functioning market economy....should be able to cope...within the EU in the near term, provided that it stays with its present reform path"
Latvia	"Continues to fulfill the Copenhagen criteria", advanced in addressing short-term priorities for accession, working on medium-term priorities; problems: administrative and judicial reform, corruption, integration of non-citizens	"Can be regarded as a functioning market economy....should be able to cope...within the EU in the medium term, provided that it completes and maintains the pace of its structural reforms"
Lithuania	"Continues to fulfill the Copenhagen criteria;" significant progress regarding short-term priorities for accession, working on medium-term priorities; problems: administrative and judicial reform, corruption	"Can be regarded as a functioning market economy....should be able to cope...within the EU in the medium term provided that it continues with the implementation of the current structural reform program and undertakes further necessary reforms"
Macedonia	Not on membership track; EU assisting in supporting progress "toward democracy"	Not on membership track; EU assisting in transformation "toward a market economy"
Romania	"Continues to fulfill the Copenhagen criteria," though EU still monitoring the situation closely; further actions required to meet short-term priorities for accession; problems: discrimination against minorities (Roma), administrative and judicial reform, high level of corruption, decisionmaking process in legislative bodies	"Cannot be considered as a functioning market economy....not able to cope...within the EU in the medium term. It has not substantially improved its economic prospects."
Slovakia	"Continues to meet [the Copenhagen criteria]", additional action needed on short-term priorities for accession; problems: administrative and judicial reform, corruption, integration of minorities (Roma)	"Can be regarded as a functioning market economy....should be able to cope...within the EU in the medium term, provided that the structural reform agenda is fully implemented and broadened to include remaining reforms"
Slovenia	"Continues to fulfill the Copenhagen criteria;" progress regarding short-term priorities for accession, working on medium-term priorities; problems: administrative and judicial reform, slow pace of denationalization	"Can be regarded as a functioning market economy....should be able to cope...within the EU in the near term, provided that it completes the remaining reforms that would increase competition in the economy"

SOURCE: Assessments of states on track toward membership taken from European Commission Reports on Progress Towards Accession, November 2000; http://europa.eu.int/comm/enlargement/index.htm. Assessments of states not on track toward membership taken from Reports on EU External

1. The highest assessment, along the lines of "fulfills the Copenhagen criteria, and has addressed all or most of the short-term accession partnership goals and is working on medium-term goals," was given to Estonia, Latvia, Lithuania, and Slovenia.

2. A lower assessment, along the lines of "fulfills the Copenhagen criteria, but still needs to address some major short-term accession partnership goals," was given to Bulgaria and Slovakia.

3. A conditional assessment, along the lines of "fulfills the Copenhagen criteria, though the EU is monitoring the situation closely, and the country still needs to address some major short-term accession partnership goals," was given to Romania.

4. The assessment that EU was "supporting progress toward democracy" was given to Macedonia and Albania, two countries not involved in accession negotiations with the EU.

Similarly, for the same nine countries, there are six distinguishable gradations in economic progress evident in the EU evaluations:

1. The highest assessment, "is a functioning market economy" and "should be able to cope with competitive pressure and market forces within the Union in the near term," was given to Estonia.

2. The next highest assessment, "can be regarded as a functioning market economy" and "should be able to cope with competitive pressure and market forces within the Union in the near term," went to Slovenia.

3. A more guarded assessment, "can be regarded as a functioning market economy" and "should be able to cope with competitive pressure and market forces within the Union in the medium term," was given to Latvia, Lithuania, and Slovakia.

4. A more conditional assessment, "has clearly made further progress toward becoming a functioning market economy" though it is "not yet able to cope with competitive pressure and market forces within the Union in the medium term," was given to Bulgaria.

5. An unsatisfactory assessment, "cannot be considered as a functioning market economy" and "is not able to cope with competi-

tive pressure and market forces within the Union in the medium term," went to Romania.

6. The assessment that the EU was aiding them in building foundations of a market economy went to Macedonia and Albania, the two countries not on the EU accession track.

Composite Assessment of Meeting Pre-Conditions

Using the assessments presented above, a scale can be constructed to match the five NATO pre-conditions for membership. These pre-conditions fall into three main categories: political, economic, and military. The political category includes criteria for a functioning democratic political system, democratic civil-military relations, and treatment of minority populations. The economic category has one criterion, that of a functioning market economy; the military category also has one criterion, military contribution to NATO.

Progress in meeting NATO's political criteria is evaluated on the basis of information derived from the Freedom House ratings and EU assessments (with the four political-assessment gradations coded as high, medium-high, medium-low, or low, with high representing the best assessment). The EU assessments pay much attention to elements of a democratic political system and minority rights, and pay less attention to civil-military relations. However, civil-military relations are not a problematic criterion for most MAP states (Albania and Macedonia are the exceptions), because NATO's thresholds for considering a state to have democratic civil-military relations are low. The three NATO members that joined in 1999 have a structure of civilian control over their armed forces that is similar in outline to that of most other NATO countries. But in fact, civilian control in the three new members remains superficial, reduced in practice to budgetary control and formal oversight, and consisting of civilian personnel only at the highest levels (due to a shortage of civilian defense specialists).[7] Since NATO views this level of civilian control as sufficient for meeting the pre-conditions (and this level is much higher than the one in Turkey, a long-standing NATO member), only those

---

[7]Stefan Sarvas, "Professional Soldiers and Politics: A Case of Central and Eastern Europe," *Armed Forces and Society*, 26:1, Fall 1999, pp. 99–118.

MAP states that fall short in their overall democratic credentials (Albania and Macedonia) fail to meet the standard.

The coding is as follows. The Freedom House country ratings are grouped into four categories based on degree of freedom attained in political rights and civil liberties: high (combined score of 2 to 3, representing the norm within NATO), medium-high (combined score of 4 to 5, still a Freedom House "free" rating), medium-low (combined score of 6 to 7, representing a "partially free" rating but close to "free" status), and low (combined score of 8 or more, meaning considerable divergence from anything resembling NATO norms). The high rating is given to Estonia, Latvia, Lithuania, Slovakia, and Slovenia; medium-high to Bulgaria and Romania; medium-low to Macedonia; and low to Albania. The EU political assessments are grouped into four categories of convergence with existing EU standards (presented earlier): high, medium-high, medium-low, and low. The high rating is given to Estonia, Latvia, Lithuania, and Slovenia; medium-high to Bulgaria and Slovakia; medium-low to Romania; and low to Macedonia and Albania. The Freedom House and EU assessments are considered to be of equal importance, and the average of the two is taken as the overall political score.

Progress in meeting NATO's economic criterion (a functioning market economy) is also evaluated on the basis of information derived from the EU assessments. In terms of coding, the six economic-assessment gradations are reduced to a four-point scale based on the time frame for the country's ability to cope with the economic pressures of being in the EU: high (near-term; Estonia and Slovenia), medium-high (medium-term; Latvia, Lithuania, and Slovakia), medium-low (beyond the medium term; Bulgaria and Romania), and low (still moving toward a market economy; Albania and Macedonia).

Progress in meeting NATO's military criterion is based on data concerning defense expenditures per troop. The use of defense expenditures per troop stems from NATO's main condition that new members be able to contribute to NATO. Since such contributions must be made in a NATO framework, only technologically sophisticated forces count. A four-point scale based on the current NATO Europe "floor" in this category (Poland, at $14,469) is used for coding. A MAP country spending higher than 25 percent more than the per-troop "floor" level ($18,086 or higher) is coded as high; such a country already exceeds several current NATO members. A MAP country spending within the 25 percent range, in either a positive or a negative direction, of the current NATO per-troop "floor" level ($10,852 to $18,085) is coded as medium-high; such a country is either at or close to the NATO "floor." A MAP country spending 25 to 50 percent less than the current NATO "floor" level ($7,235 to $10,851) is coded as medium-low. A MAP country spending less than 50 percent of the current NATO per-troop "floor" level is coded as low. A high rating is given to Slovenia; medium-high to Estonia; medium-low to Latvia, Lithuania, Macedonia, and Slovakia; and low to Albania, Bulgaria, and Romania.

The criterion for resolution of disputes with neighboring countries is not taken into account. This is a simple yes or no assessment, and all of the aspiring members in the early and medium groups have resolved such disputes in the course of being placed on the membership track.[8]

Each assessment is then assigned a numerical score, ranging from 1 for low to 4 for high. Since the political assessment includes two indicators, the two are averaged. An overall assessment, both numerical and using a three-point (low, medium, high) scale can then be presented. Table 4.16 presents the composite ratings for the nine recognized aspirants.

The ratings in Table 4.16 and the assessments of defense expenditures and extent of political and economic transition presented earlier have some common themes:

---

[8]Estonia and Latvia each have a boundary with Russia that has not been settled conclusively in a legal sense. Both of these countries have expressed their readiness to sign treaties codifying the current border, but Russia has been reluctant to sign. Given the circumstances, both states meet the criterion of being committed to settling disputes peacefully and legally. As for Albania and Macedonia, they still need to settle their relations with neighboring states, but that problem simply compounds their overall low ratings in all categories.

Table 4.16

**Overall Assessments of Extent to Which MAP States Meet
Declared NATO Criteria**

State	Political[a]	Economic[a]	Military[a]	Total[b]	Overall Assessment[c]
Albania	Low (1)	Low (1)	Low (1)	3	0.0 (Low)
Bulgaria	Medium-high (3)	Medium-low (2)	Low (1)	6	3.3 (Medium)
Estonia	High (4)	High (4)	Medium-high (3)	11	8.9 (High)
Latvia	High (4)	Medium-high (3)	Medium-low (2)	9	6.7 (Medium
Lithuania	High (4)	Medium-high (3)	Medium-low (2)	9	6.7 (Medium)
Macedonia	Low to medium-low (1.5)	Low (1)	Medium-low (2)	4.5	1.7 (Low)
Romania	Medium (2.5)	Medium-low (2)	Low (1)	5.5	2.8 (Low)
Slovakia	Medium-high to high (3.5)	Medium-high (3)	Medium-low (2)	8.5	6.2 (Medium)
Slovenia	High (4)	High (4)	High (4)	12	10.0 (High)

SOURCE: Assessments presented earlier.

[a]Scale in political, economic, and military categories: low = 1; medium-low = 2; medium-high = 3; high = 4.

[b]The scores for the political, economic, and military categories were added together for an overall possible total from a minimum of 3 to a maximum of 12. The resulting 9-point scale was converted to a 0–10 scale (for purposes of cross-comparison carried out later in the chapter). For example, Bulgaria's total of 6 translates into 3.3 on a 0–10 scale.

[c]Overall assessment ranged from a minimum of 0 to a maximum of 10; the resulting 11-point scale was divided into three sections, with the middle section being the largest (distribution is 30%, 40%, 30%). The overall section was coded in the following manner: 0–3 = low; 3.1–6.9 = medium; 7–10 = high.

1. Slovenia meets all the criteria established by NATO, earning a "high" ranking in each of the three categories for assessment. Although the small size of its military limits the overall contribution it might make to NATO in an absolute sense, its high per-troop defense spending suggests a military that could fit easily into NATO.

2. Estonia follows, meeting the political and economic criteria. The small size of its military limits its contribution to NATO, and it is still below, though close to, the NATO "floor" level in indicators of the quality of its armed forces.

3. Latvia, Lithuania, and Slovakia are not far behind, with some shortfalls in meeting the economic criteria. However, their main

shortcomings are in the military realm, with constraints evident in the quality of their armed forces.

4. Bulgaria and especially Romania fall substantially short of meeting the pre-conditions and have problems in all three areas.

5. Macedonia and especially Albania need to make substantial progress before they can be considered seriously for NATO membership.

6. The EU members currently not in NATO easily meet NATO's criteria, although Austria would need to raise its defense spending.

A similar assessment, using 1997–99 data and concerning the three countries that joined NATO in 1999, indicates that all three new members scored in the high category overall. However, in 1997–99, Slovenia was in the same "high" category as these three and yet failed to be invited. That failure points out the importance of the strategic rationale used by NATO in its enlargement plans, a rationale that is dealt with next.

STRATEGIC RATIONALE

The composite assessment does not determine which countries NATO will invite to join. A crucial element of the decisionmaking process is the strategic rationale for inviting a particular country to join. A strategic assessment entails looking at the costs and benefits of including a new member in NATO in terms of two key issues: strategic position and armed forces. *Strategic position* refers to the impact a new member will have on NATO's main missions; *armed forces* refers to the additional requirements for military forces that the enlargement would entail and the extent to which these requirements would be offset by the new member's military contribution to NATO.

Strategic Position

If NATO's future evolution accords with the 1999 Strategic Concept, then NATO will continue to focus on the dominant mission of power projection for conflict management and conflict prevention and the residual mission of collective defense of members' territory. The strategic costs and benefits to NATO from further enlargement, as they pertain to both missions, can be assessed along the following dimensions:

- The ability to project power unhindered in areas of likely contingencies.

- The creation of interior and easily defensible borders within NATO (and the avoidance of long and exposed borders that need to be defended at added cost).

- Risks that may accrue from a higher commitment to a new ally.

- NATO's cohesion and its ability to perform its main missions on the basis of consensus.

Each of these issues is explored below.

In examining strategic costs and benefits, this report does not attempt to project the expenditures connected with adding any specific MAP country to NATO. As the debate over the 1997–99 round of enlargement showed, the costs of enlargement are highly susceptible to becoming grossly inflated if worst-case assumptions come into play. Such assumptions, which entail a fundamental change in the security environment, are plausible only in an unexpected-shock situation, not a situation that entails only shifts in emphasis or a no-surprises future. This report assumes that strategic choices will drive enlargement and that the specific costs of force development will follow from those choices. If there should be a fundamental change in the security environment, even enormous costs thought wholly unacceptable in a no-surprises future could be judged worthy of pursuit. This report assumes a no-surprises future, that NATO will not expend additional resources on enlargement per se (other than some infrastructure improvement efforts), and that the actual direct costs of enlargement (adjustment and adaptation) will be borne primarily by new members. Current members may have to bear the costs of altering their armed forces to make them suitable for power projection missions, but these costs fall under NATO's transformation, not its enlargement. In addition, NATO has decided to proceed with enlargement at a pace that entails few additional costs.[9] Under the conditions of a continued benign security environment, this situation is likely to continue. Other than opportunity costs, which are related to strategic choices (and considered in the third point of the preceding paragraph), the direct costs of enlargement most likely will be covered by adjustments and transfers from existing appropriations. In other words, further enlargement will not require any net increases of non-trivial size over and above projected levels of defense outlays.

Power Projection. What is the cost-benefit calculus connected with NATO's ability to project power unhindered in areas of likely contingencies? The geographical focus of the power projection missions is the Balkans. NATO has engaged in coercive peacemaking in former Yugoslavia (Bosnia-Herzegovina and Kosovo) and has assisted Albania and Macedonia in securing their sovereignty. NATO's presence and level of effort may even deepen and expand over the next 10 to 15 years because of the largely weak and transitioning states in the Balkans and in view of certain "branch-point" contingencies coming to pass. The Mediterranean littoral[10] and eastern Europe[11] are other areas where NATO may become involved in peace operations over the next 10 to 15 years (again, depending on the branch-point contingencies). However, both areas are distinctly secondary to NATO's main Balkan involvement in the near- and mid-term.

NATO has been reluctant to engage in peace operations in areas of the former USSR because Russia, a country with which NATO needs to maintain a cooperative relationship, would likely respond negatively to NATO's doing so. This trend is likely to persist under conditions of no major shocks to the security environment. Under some branch-point developments, however, scenarios might plausibly develop in which NATO could become drawn into a greater peacekeep-

---

[9]For a good presentation of the pros and cons of the various estimates and an alternative, zero-net-cost proposal (followed, more or less, in practice), see Reiner K. Huber and Gernot Friedrich, *A Zero-Cost Option for NATO Enlargement: Arguments for a Comprehensive Approach*, The Potomac Papers, McLean, Virginia, August 1997.

[10]Ian O. Lesser, *NATO Looks South: New Challenges and New Strategies in the Mediterranean*, RAND, MR-1126-AF, 2000.

[11]The term *eastern Europe* is used here in its geographical meaning and refers primarily to the European portions of the former Soviet Union.

ing, or at least humanitarian, role in areas such as Moldova. From the perspective of a transformed NATO's missions for the next decade and beyond, though, the Balkans is an area of primary strategic importance.

NATO's collective defense mission remains focused on NATO's eastern borders for the simple reason that almost all of NATO's land borders with non-NATO countries are to its east, making that area the only possible site for a conventional military threat. Other potential contingencies involve ballistic missile proliferation and hypothetical threats that Islamist fundamentalists in northern Africa and the Middle East may pose to southern European members or to Turkey. However, the only conventional military threat that NATO sees as potential would come by way of an unexpected political shock in Russia and an end to cooperative NATO-Russian relations.

Assuming the continuing focus of NATO's conflict prevention and conflict management efforts in the Balkans for the near- and mid-term, membership for some aspiring countries would improve the situation for any future contingencies involving Serbia by raising the level of confidence for basing and airspace use. In the Kosovo operation, NATO relied on non-members to open their airspace for NATO air operations in order to gain tactical surprise and use all avenues of attack on Serbia proper. However, extending NATO membership does not necessarily guarantee such access. During the Kosovo operation, several aspiring members—Romania, Bulgaria, Slovenia, and Slovakia—opened their airspace for all NATO air operations. In contrast, Austria—a non-NATO EU member—and Greece—a longstanding NATO member—did not. Such experience leads to the question of whether NATO secures more-effective rights to basing and airspace use from members or from countries aspiring to be members. It could be argued that aspiring members make more-reliable partners because cooperating with NATO keeps their chances for membership on track.

There are several problems with such an argument, however. Consider, for example, how NATO membership might affect Romania and Bulgaria during coercive peace operations centering on Serbia. Under the conditions of no unexpected shocks, Romania and Bulgaria, as members of NATO, would have no reason to follow the pro-Serbian proclivities of Greece, the only country near Serbia to maintain such a position. Instead, they would be more likely to exhibit behavior akin to that of Hungary and Turkey during any Kosovo-like operations, for the following reason. Romania and Bulgaria's security motivations, important in driving their NATO aspirations, would lead them, as NATO members, to attempt to prove their worth as allies in an actual NATO operation so as to ensure strong commitment from other allies of assistance in the event that they (Romania and Bulgaria) were to face threats in the future. In other words, these countries would not want to be perceived as free riders. The same incentives that led Romania to open its airspace to NATO air operations during the Kosovo operation would remain securely in place if Romania were a NATO member, as long as Romania's governing elite continues to perceive Romania as insecure in the face of potential future military threats. Moreover, membership entails greater progress in interoperability than non-membership does. As a result, cooperation with other member states is likely to be more effective prior to and during any future peace operation in the Balkans, thus raising the level of overall NATO effectiveness.

Returning to the question posed at the beginning of this section on power projection, an assessment can now be made of how effectively the membership of specific countries would improve NATO's ability to project power unhindered in areas of likely contingencies. In terms of increasing the effectiveness of possible future NATO peace operations in the main area of potential operations, the Balkans (and without addressing the other criteria), NATO would benefit from the membership of Austria, Slovakia, Slovenia, Bulgaria, Romania, Albania, and Macedonia, and would not benefit from the membership of Latvia, Lithuania, Estonia, Sweden, or Finland.

Interior Borders. What is the cost-benefit calculus connected with creating interior borders within NATO? In the context of NATO's residual collective defense mission, costs can be saved by limiting the length of borders that need to be defended, which reduces the number of forces required and the costs these forces entail. Borders requiring fewer forces for their defense because of natural obstacles such as mountain ranges are desirable and modify the length calculations. Conversely, long and exposed land borders requiring defense increase the need for covering forces and increase costs to NATO. In terms of NATO enlargement, adding a new member that shortens NATO's borders with non-members is beneficial and, all other things being equal, adding a member that lengthens NATO's borders with non-members is not beneficial. It is important to note here, however, that a cost-benefit calculation based on cost savings from interior borders did not sway the decisionmaking in NATO's 1997–99 round of accession. The inclusion of Hungary, a non-contiguous member, shows the low relevance of the collective defense mission to the 1997–99 decision.

The merits of further NATO enlargement on the basis of cost-benefit calculations stemming from interior borders were examined recently at length using game theory.[12] The results support the intuitive conclusion that NATO would realize substantial cost savings from the membership of Austria, Slovakia, and Slovenia. All other things being equal, it would not realize cost savings, however, from adding countries that are contiguous to NATO but elongate its border—i.e., Romania, Lithuania, Bulgaria, Macedonia, Albania, Sweden, and Finland.[13] The most costly and least beneficial option would be to include a non-contiguous country such as Latvia or Estonia. These calculations are based on single-country accessions. The calculus changes if certain countries join simultaneously, sometimes making the accessions less costly but never changing the overall results given above. For example, a joint Bulgarian and Romanian accession would not be as costly as having Romania join alone.

New Risks. What is the cost-benefit calculus connected with the risks that may accrue to NATO from a higher commitment to a new ally? The inclusion of a new member could bring into play at least three types of risks: (1) NATO could be drawn into an otherwise avoidable bilateral dispute; (2) making the commitment to the new member real could entail opportunity costs that would cause NATO to forgo other, more important initiatives; (3) the overall security environment could be negatively affected.

The first risk—having a new member entangle NATO in an international dispute that otherwise could be avoided—is an unnecessary cost. For example, if added security and a perception of being in a

---

[12]Todd Sandler, "Alliance Formation, Alliance Expansion, and the Core," *Journal of Conflict Resolution*, 43:6, December 1999, pp. 727–747.

[13]Ibid., p. 742.

stronger position because of NATO membership were to encourage the new member to take actions that aggravate an existing dispute or initiate a new dispute, other NATO countries would be "chain ganged," i.e., trapped and led into tensions or conflict by an ally's behavior. However, if inclusion of a new member were to improve the status of an existing NATO dispute, the move would be beneficial to NATO. Having a new member that fits neither option is a neutral result.

As to the second point, every new member entails some costs to NATO to make the commitment real, even if the costs are minimal and limited to those needed to bring the new member's infrastructure in line with NATO specifications. But other costs must also be considered in this category—i.e., those connected with possible actions NATO could take but, because of its attention to and payment for making the commitment real, does not. Opportunity costs can be limited if inclusion of a new member follows the course of actions that NATO would carry out anyway. If, however, the inclusion follows a largely separate track from NATO's general activities and detracts from other, potentially more fruitful activities, the move would not be beneficial.

Regarding the third issue, and related to both of the preceding points, NATO is most interested in continuing the current benign security environment through proactive shaping in the unintegrated area of Europe. If inclusion of a new member significantly worsens the overall security environment, then, all other things being equal, the move is not beneficial, because it entails costs potentially far and above the benefits that an addition of any one new member might bring.

Where do the various aspiring members stand with regard to drawing NATO into an otherwise avoidable bilateral dispute? To a certain extent, NATO has attempted to eliminate this problem through its pre-condition that all prospective members settle any bilateral disputes with neighboring countries. As noted earlier, this requirement has improved the security environment in central and southern Europe, where the possibility of accession to NATO is perceived to be real. Our examination of potential disputes is limited to those that might emerge under a continuation of current trends in the security environment. If a major and unexpected political shock were to occur, then almost by definition, some long-dormant or seemingly set-tled bilateral problems would arise. For example, if Russia were to break up or the EU to unravel, all kinds of systemic uncertainties with high local consequences would prevail. Attempting even to forecast the likely pathways that could result from such low-proba-bility and high-consequence events would lead to a voluminous list of worst-case scenarios, something that clarifies little of the issues at hand.

In the early group of NATO aspirants, Slovakia and Slovenia have no obvious bilateral disputes that might emerge after their accession if the existing security trends in Europe continue. If anything, Slovak-Hungarian ties are likely to improve as a consequence of both coun-tries being integrated into NATO.

In the middle group of NATO aspirants, Lithuania has no outstand-ing bilateral problems with its neighbors, and Bulgaria seems un-likely to import new disputes into NATO since its sometimes tense relations with Serbia fit into the overall pattern of NATO-Serbian re-lations. As for Romania, its ties to Moldova are the only ones that may cause future complications. Rather than conflict, however, the Romanian-Moldovan relations could become problematic under branch-point scenarios of Moldova becoming a "failed state" and Romania perceiving a need to assist its co-ethnics in Moldova.[14] Because of the unsolved issue of trans-Dniester secessionism (with Russian collusion), the greater drawing of Romania into Moldovan affairs could become problematic in terms of Romanian-Russian re-lations. However, it is not clear that Romania's entry into NATO would be detrimental or beneficial to NATO in case of a state failure in Moldova, since under such conditions, NATO is likely to be in-volved in support of humanitarian relief operations in Moldova anyway.

---

[14]Vlada Tkach, "Moldova and Transdniestria: Painful Past, Deadlocked Present, Uncertain Future," *European Security*, 8:2, Summer 1999, pp. 130–159; John O'Loughlin, Vladimir Kolossov, and Andrei Tchepalyga, "National Construction, Territorial Separatism, and Post-Soviet Geopolitics in the Transdniester Moldovan Republic," *Post-Soviet Geography and Economics*, 39:6, June 1998, pp. 332–358; Nina Orlova and Per Ronnas, "The Crippling Cost of an Incomplete Transformation: The Case of Moldova," *Post-Communist Economies*, 11:3, September 1999, pp. 373–398.

Latvia and Estonia have a border with Russia that is not settled conclusively even though both countries have abandoned their previous legalistic claims to parts of Russia (small parts of pre-1940 eastern Latvia and Estonia that the Soviet regime unilaterally transferred to the Russian Socialist Federated Soviet Republic in 1947, after annexing both countries to the USSR).[15] The problem lies on the Russian side and what appears to be Russia's attempt to complicate Estonia and Latvia's ability to meet NATO's pre-conditions.[16] The position of the Russian minority in both Latvia and Estonia is also a bilateral problem, though it is primarily a problem magnified by Russia.[17] Internally, in both countries, the position of the Russian minority has been monitored closely by the OSCE Human Rights Commissioner. So far, the OSCE verdict has been that the conditions of the minority fit the general OSCE principles. Moreover, there has been little indication that the Russian minorities in either country have been unhappy over the last decade, as evidenced by their lack of ethnic activism and their negligible rate of migration to Russia.

In the long-term group of NATO aspirants, both Albania and Macedonia need to establish viable and fully functioning state structures[18] before tackling semi-dormant issues of bilateral disputes and, in the case of Albania, deciding on a policy toward Macedonia and Kosovo. Finally, none of the current non-NATO EU members has outstanding bilateral problems that, under assumptions of a

---

[15]Estonia had claimed the eastern bank of the Narva river and the Petseri/Pechory region in what is now the western part of Russia's Pskov province. Latvia had claimed the Abrene region, or what is now the western part (Pytalovo and surrounding areas) of Russia's Pskov region.

[16]Mark A. Cichock, "Interdependence and Manipulation in the Russian-Baltic Relationship: 1993-97," *Journal of Baltic Studies*, 30:2, Summer 1999, pp. 89–116; Wayne C. Thompson, "Citizenship and Borders: Legacies of Soviet Empire in Estonia," *Journal of Baltic Studies*, 29:2, Summer 1998, pp. 109–134.

[17]A theoretically well-grounded study of the Russophone populations in the non-Russian successor states of the USSR points to Latvia and Estonia as having the best conditions for peaceful accommodation and assimilation of the Russophones and indicates that these processes are already under way. David D. Laitin, *Identity in Formation: The Russian-Speaking Populations in the Near Abroad*, Ithaca, NY: Cornell University Press, 1998.

[18]Paul Kubicek, "Another Balkan Humpty-Dumpty: Putting Albania Back Together," *European Security*, 7:2, Summer 1998, pp. 78–91; Fabian Schmidt, "Enemies Far and Near: Macedonia's Fragile Stability," *Problems of Post-Communism*, 45:4, July-August 1998, pp. 22–31.

continuation of existing security trends, might draw NATO into a new dispute.

All in all, other than Latvia and Estonia's problems with Russia, there are no clear bilateral problems that would lead NATO into a new dispute as a result of admitting any of the aspiring members examined above. (Albania and Macedonia are exceptions, but their membership prospects are not viable in the short- and mid-term.) Latvia and Estonia's problems with Russia stem from Russian unwillingness to settle the border issue and Russian activism on behalf of Latvia and Estonia's Russian minorities, rather than from any intransigence by Latvia or Estonia. However, the situation could become exacerbated if Russia were to use the bilateral problems as leverage to keep the two countries from joining NATO.

What kind of opportunity costs does the accession of aspiring members entail? In terms of NATO's main focus on conflict prevention and conflict management and its geographical focus on the Balkans, NATO's presence in Albania and Macedonia has led to an upgrade of these two countries' transport infrastructures, such as air traffic control and road and rail networks. A multitude of road and rail projects are also being implemented in Slovakia, Slovenia, Romania, and Bulgaria as part of a long-term EU plan to assist these countries in joining the EU. Many of these programs are funded or supported by the EU or other European institutions. On a lesser scale, similar programs have been designed for Lithuania, Latvia, and Estonia. Improvements in air traffic control in all the NATO aspirants have been implemented since the mid-1990s with European (Eurocontrol) and U.S. assistance (growing out of the Warsaw Initiative). The regional Air Sovereignty Operations Centers (ASOCs) linked to the new air traffic control systems are interoperable with NATO early warning and, in theory, with integrated air defense systems. Through PfP, NATO has assisted all the aspiring members in making some of their air bases suitable for use by NATO aircraft.

Thus, the question of cost for infrastructure improvements that might be needed to make a military commitment real to the aspiring members depends on the time frame adopted. If the improvements had to be made rapidly in the next few years, the costs would be nontrivial. However, in a 10 to 15 year time frame, the costs will be lower because at least a rudimentary expressway and heavy train infrastructure will be in place for all the aspiring members. An earlier schedule is projected for air traffic control and preparation of select air bases in the aspiring states. As of late 2000, the MAP states were close to becoming integrated into the NATO-compatible civil-military air traffic control system and could be tied easily to the integrated NATO air defense system.

In view of NATO's focus on and operations in the Balkans and the extensive work carried out since 1996 in the region to support NATO operations, the entry of Slovakia, Slovenia, Bulgaria, Romania, Albania, and Macedonia would not entail substantial additional costs over what NATO already has spent or intends to spend in order to make the membership real. Since 1996, NATO has carried out detailed surveys of airfields and assisted in preparing some airfields in the aspiring countries for NATO use. In terms of road and rail infrastructure, a faster pace of implementation for the EU-sponsored regional transportation network would entail greater outlays by NATO. The above assumes the continuation of current security trends, with no immediate threat that would force NATO into a massive overhaul of infrastructure.

NATO's current relatively low involvement in the eastern Baltic littoral (Lithuania, Latvia, and Estonia) means that NATO investment in a rapid buildup of infrastructure to make membership commitment real to these three countries would entail siphoning funds from another priority. However, by 2015, existing EU plans, if implemented, will complete all the infrastructure improvements that NATO conceivably might consider in the short-term.

What kind of impact would the accession of aspiring members have on the security environment? By far the most important aspect of this question is how Russia will react, because Russia is the only country in Europe that objects to NATO's enlargement.[19] Absent Russian objections, accession would be non-controversial and subject only to NATO's deciding to invite some countries as members. If the existing security trends continue, NATO is likely to continue

---

[19]The current regime in Belarus also objects to NATO's enlargement, but its objections are based on its policy toward Russia. In any event, it is not clear that a non-authoritarian regime in Belarus would treat NATO's enlargement in a way different from Ukraine.

paying much attention to enlargement's impact on Russia. Russia may not be able to stop further enlargement, but it could change the European security environment for the worse, whether in eastern Europe or in the Balkans. Since NATO's transformation and enlargement have the larger goal of keeping the current benign security environment in place, calculations of NATO's further enlargement must consider the potential for less-cooperative Russian behavior.

In principle, Russian officials continue to object to any further enlargement of NATO, whether that means accession of Sweden, Bulgaria, or Slovenia. Nonetheless, there is wide variance in the likely Russian reactions to different countries' accession. The general pattern is as follows: the closer the country is to Russia, the larger its military potential is, and the greater its level of integration with the USSR was in the Soviet era, the greater the likelihood that the country's accession to NATO will cause a negative Russian reaction that will have an impact on the overall security environment in Europe.

Russia appears to have accepted the fact that the remaining three former Warsaw Pact satellites eventually will join NATO, just as four have done already. Russia accepted, if grudgingly, the accession of East Germany and then Poland, the Czech Republic, and Hungary as part of a bargaining process with NATO without disrupting the overall security environment. The same result can be reasonably expected as a consequence of bargaining over the accession of Slovakia, Romania, and Bulgaria, especially since these countries are much less central than Poland or eastern Germany in Russian security thinking.

Russian objections to the possibility of the accession of former communist countries not a part of the Warsaw Pact have been distinctly less vociferous. Even in 1997, Russian officials did not object to Slovenia joining NATO. It is difficult to speculate about their reaction to a near- or mid-term accession of Albania and Macedonia, however, because they have not commented on the issue, probably because it seems implausible to them. Russian officials do continue to object to Austria, Sweden, and Finland acceding to NATO, with Finland's potential accession being in a league of its own because of Finland's proximity to Russian population centers, its long border with Russia, and its formerly close relations with the USSR.

Russia has drawn a line against the accession of countries that used to be annexed outright to the USSR. This means that the accession of Lithuania, Latvia, and Estonia in the near- and perhaps mid-term would likely be detrimental to the overall security environment because of the effect it would have on Russian attitudes. Under current security trends and in view of Russia's admonitions and threats (including military) against such a move, the accession of any or all of these countries would be possible only if accompanied by an acceptable (and probably extensive) "compensation" to Russia.

It is important to differentiate between Russian rhetoric meant to influence NATO decisionmaking and Russian pragmatism once NATO has made a decision. For example, Russia engaged in a campaign of threats and intimidation in 1997 during the run-up to NATO's membership invitations to Poland, the Czech Republic, and Hungary. Russia warned against the move but ultimately could do nothing to stop it and agreed to enlargement in the course of negotiations with NATO. Evidence from NATO's enlargement in 1997–99 suggests that it had little visible impact on the Russian internal political situation or on Russian relations with the main NATO countries. As one observer of Russian foreign policy noted:

> In 1996–1997, as the West pushed ahead with NATO expansion and expanded links with some of Russia's neighbors, there was no noticeable increase in the political fortunes of Russian hard-liners. On the contrary, in 1997, the Russian government became more reform-oriented at home and backed away from confrontation with the West on foreign policy. . . . When the West adopts a unified policy that will brook no Russian opposition (as in Bosnia and in NATO expansion), Russia backs down from rhetorical threats and tries to save face by getting the best deal it can at a negotiating table.[20]

As the above makes clear, further enlargement will entail "compensation" to Russia because Russia opposes enlargement in principle and can worsen the overall security environment if the "compensation" is insufficient, but it would be imprudent for NATO to allow Russian rhetoric to affect its decisions. The "compensation" may be miniscule and symbolic, as in the case of Slovenia, or exten-

---

[20]Paul Kubicek, "Russian Foreign Policy and the West," *Political Science Quarterly,* 114:4, 1999–2000, p. 567.

sive and subject to far-reaching negotiations, as in the case of Lithuania, Latvia, Estonia, or Finland. Theoretically, NATO could press for Lithuania, Latvia, and Estonia's inclusion in NATO. If unified on the issue and willing to bargain with Russia, NATO would probably succeed without irreparably damaging Russia's willingness to cooperate. Nonetheless, this proposition begs the question of what benefits would accrue to NATO in exchange for the substantial political costs it would pay for the move. NATO's Parliamentary Assembly has noted this point explicitly:

> In the final analysis, the point is that enlargement is a means to an end, and not an end in itself. If rapid enlargement reduces the security environment of the Euro-Atlantic area, then it is better to wait, despite the aspirations of the applicant states.[21]

Transaction Costs. What is the cost-benefit calculus connected with NATO's growth as it relates to NATO's cohesion and its ability to perform its main missions on the basis of consensus? Simple mathematics indicates that the greater the number of decisionmakers, the more difficult it is to reach consensus. Moreover, the level of difficulty does not increase in a linear manner. A larger membership also entails greater costs for gathering information and coordinating joint efforts aimed at interoperability. Finally, the greater the membership and the greater the differentiation among members, the more potential there is for free riding, non-compliance, and selective participation. These problems are not new for NATO; in fact, they have existed as long as NATO has, though their form has evolved over the course of several decades.

But the simple mathematical calculation just described obfuscates some deeper issues involving NATO's dynamics. The important question concerns the extent to which member countries maintain a common vision of security and develop bonds to facilitate cooperation within NATO. The NATO Europe states are linked by more than an integrated military structure led by the United States. Treating these states as fiercely independent entities competitive with each other misses the most important development of the second half of

---

[21]NATO Parliamentary Assembly, Political Committee, Sub-Committee on NATO Enlargement and the New Democracies, *NATO-Russia Relations and Next Steps for NATO Enlargement*, Peter Viggers (rapporteur), September 28, 1999, paragraph 42.

the 20th century: the emergence of supra-national bonds in Europe. As a result of several decades of European integration, NATO's major European members are integrated politically, economically, and socially to an extent not formerly witnessed in modern history, and they have the same or similar economic interests vis-à-vis non-EU countries. EU membership is largely coterminous with European NATO membership, and the fact that these two organizations have similar lists of enlargement candidates means that their memberships will remain coterminous in the future. Different views toward specific security issues do persist within NATO, often stemming from a simple matter of geography or the position of a given country's ruling coalition on the ideological spectrum. Nonetheless, to concentrate on these differences is to miss the more important and remarkable point—the similarity of the European NATO members' views on security.[22] This shared vision is borne out by Operation Allied Force, for which 17 European states agreed to engage in extensive military operations and risk casualties because of humanitarian concerns—by definition a discretionary rationale for use of force.

In conditions of a benign security environment coupled with continuing and deepening EU integration, the potential danger that further enlargement poses to NATO cohesion is relevant only when the potential new member does not share the European integrationist outlook. The general pattern to be expected is that the greater the new NATO member's economic and political integration in the EU,

---

[22]There is strong evidence that the domestic political systems of the members of an alliance make a great deal of difference for cohesion within an alliance. Empirical tests of alliances since 1815 show that adding democratic members to an alliance, even after controlling for a variety of factors, decreases the probability of alliance failure. The likely reason is that with increasing numbers of democratic members, "audience costs" are imposed on all members. (Kurt Taylor Gaubatz, "Democratic States and Commitment in International Relations," *International Organization*, 50:1, Winter 1996, pp. 109–139; William Reed, "Alliance Duration and Democracy: An Extension and Cross-Validation of 'Democratic States and Commitment in International Relations,'" *American Journal of Political Science*, 41:3, July 1997, pp. 1072–1078; Brett Ashley Leeds, "Domestic Political Institutions, Credible Commitments, and International Cooperation, *American Journal of Political Science*, 43:4, October 1999, pp. 979–1002.) In any event, opinions in the major NATO countries (both elite and popular levels) regarding the challenges NATO is facing are surprising for their consensus; see the country chapters in Michael Brenner, ed., *NATO and Collective Security*, New York: St. Martin's Press, Inc., 1998.

the less likely that member is to pose substantial problems for NATO cohesion.

The early and middle groups of NATO aspirants are on track to EU membership and conduct the majority of their trade with EU countries. Based on when the initial invitations were issued and the EU's latest assessment of the progress toward accession that the prospective members have made so far, Estonia and Slovenia may enter the EU in 2003–05, followed later by Latvia, Slovakia, and Lithuania. Bulgaria and Romania are longer-term candidates for EU membership, while Macedonia and Albania are not yet on a membership track. The above groupings largely correspond to the likely extent of cohesion problems that these countries' membership would pose for NATO. The longer a potential NATO member is a member of the EU before acceding to NATO, the less likely its accession is to cause problems of cohesion for NATO. From such a perspective, current EU members not in NATO would pose few problems for NATO's cohesion.

Armed Forces

The defense expenditures of aspiring NATO members were discussed earlier as one of the pre-conditions for membership. At this point, we need to take a more detailed look at the armed forces of these countries to perform the strategic calculations regarding the costs and benefits of accession. The starting point for this strategic analysis is NATO's rejection of any formal differentiation between long-standing and recent members, which means that the responsibilities and missions of new members will be the same as those of current members. Foremost, these responsibilities include each member's ability to provide for the defense of its own territory: it must keep intact a credible deterrent to aggression by providing an effective initial defense of its own borders. If threatened, it can rely on assistance from allies for reinforcement, with the size of the reinforcing forces depending on the aggressor. Under the conditions of a continuation of the current benign security environment, calculations of the necessary deterrent force are purely theoretical. However, for some plausible contingencies, NATO may need to deter aggression by deploying forces to the territory of a threatened or intimidated ally. In any case, the size and quality of a new member's forces enter the calculations regarding the size of the forces needed to reinforce that country in a crisis.

If a new member is to be a net contributor to NATO's power projection operations, its armed forces must be adequate for such a mission in both size and quality. Forces configured for power projection constitute a suitable contribution to the defense of other members, another responsibility that goes with membership in NATO and the commitment to collective defense. In view of NATO's transformation and its primary focus on power projection, new members will be expected to participate in NATO's peace operations. The lighter expeditionary-style forces appropriate for such missions are also suitable for assisting other members with collective defense and could rapidly reinforce the threatened sections of a member's own country in the event of an unexpected crisis. In the future, a member's contribution to collective defense should be a building block for that member's contribution to NATO's stability and power projection operations.

Missions of home defense and power projection both involve strategic costs and benefits to NATO in terms of further enlargement. These costs and benefits need to be assessed along the following dimensions:

1. The sufficiency of a member's forces for basic deterrence and border defense under conditions of capability planning.
2. The ability of a member's forces to contribute to NATO's power projection missions.

Distinctions along both dimensions are made here in terms of quality and quantity of forces.

Power Projection Missions. How do the aspiring members rate in terms of their ability to contribute to NATO's power projection missions? This issue deals with NATO's current primary mission of conflict management and conflict resolution and is likely to be a crucial indicator of whether a new member contributes to the alliance in a representative fashion. Addressing this question requires that the aspiring members' forces be categorized as to quality and quantity.

A simple matrix can be constructed using peacetime active forces as a measure of size, and per-troop annual expenditures as a measure of technological sophistication. The matrix produces four categories among the new members and recognized aspirants: (1) countries with more-modern and large armed forces, (2) countries with less-modern and large armed forces, (3) countries with more-modern and small armed forces, and (4) countries with less-modern and small armed forces. The threshold for differentiating between more- and less-modern forces generally follows the formula used in the preceding section to establish a MAP country's ability to meet NATO's preconditions, and is based on a country's proximity to minimum current NATO standards, as exemplified by the NATO country currently spending the lowest amount of defense expenditures per troop within NATO—namely, Poland. Since Polish levels are currently at $14,469 per troop, any country coming within 25 percent of this figure ($10,852) can be said to be near the minimum NATO standards and thus is placed in the more-modern category of MAP states.

The threshold for differentiating between large and small forces is based on the country's potential contribution to NATO power projection missions. Assume that a significant contribution to NATO operations would consist of a brigade-size force. Then, keeping in mind the need for support troops, the effects of rotation and replacement schedules, and the fact that only a portion (at maximum effort, no more than a third) of a country's combat force can be detached for NATO power projection missions, the result is that a peacetime force of at least 25,000 would be needed. A smaller peacetime force is likely to contribute less than a brigade, even at maximum effort (under conditions of a continued benign security environment and thus an absence of full mobilization). The figure of 25,000 approximates Denmark's peacetime force size. Any force below that is considered "small." Figure 4.1 presents the results.

All other things being equal, NATO is most interested in countries that contribute large and modern armed forces. When Poland, the Czech Republic, and Hungary joined NATO in 1999, they were in the large and more-modern category, compared to then NATO "floor" levels (Turkey). No MAP country is currently in that category, as Figure 4.1 shows. The MAP countries' forces are either small in size

RANDMR1243-4.1

Size	More modern	Less modern
Large		Albania[a,d] Bulgaria[a,d] Romania[a,d] Slovakia[d]
Small	Estonia[c] Slovenia[b,c]	Latvia[c] Lithuania Macedonia

SOURCE: Table 4.5.

[a]Very low on modernization scale, less than 50% ($7,235 or less) of threshold ($14,469).
[b]Very high on modernization scale, more than 50% ($21,704 or more) of threshold ($14,469).
[c]Very low on size scale, less than 50% (12,500 or less) of threshold (25,000).
[d]Very high on size scale, more than 50% (37,500 or more) of threshold (25,000).

Figure 4.1—Modernization and Size Matrix

or less modern or both. Several countries (Albania, Bulgaria, and Romania) are in the least attractive category of being very low on the modernization scale and very high on the size scale. For comparison purposes, EU members currently not in NATO (with the exception of Ireland) all fall into the category of more-modern and large.

Three countries stand out favorably in this categorization. Slovakia has less-modern armed forces, though not by a radical (less than 50 percent of current NATO "floor") margin. It also has forces of not insignificant size. Slovenia has small armed forces, but its high per-troop spending levels make the quality of its forces of interest to NATO. Estonia's very small force size is offset somewhat by its proximity to current NATO "floor" levels in terms of modernization. The other aspiring members come out less favorably. Beyond the likely equipment problems (both in terms of serviceability and technological sophistication), the low per-troop spending levels are indicative of insufficient training. Thus, even if a country can contribute light infantry (thus bypassing most of the equipment problems), the training and discipline of those troops may not be adequate for NATO operations. Some, but not all, of these training problems could be mitigated by the country's contributing elite light infantry or special forces units. The above also holds true in cases where NATO provides communications equipment and vehicles to such a unit.

Deterrence Sufficiency. How do the aspiring members rate in terms of their forces' sufficiency for basic deterrence and border defense? This issue concerns NATO's residual collective defense mission. Although this mission is currently secondary to power projection, every member needs a credible deterrent so that neighbors will not be tempted to use force. Capability planning provides a standard way to assess a country's sufficiency for deterrence purposes, but it would entail calculating ratios of tanks, armored combat vehicles (ACVs), and artillery per kilometer of border that would need to be defended; identifying natural obstacles and avenues of approach; and assessing force quality in terms of training, serviceability of equipment, mobility, and infrastructure within the country that allows for rapid deployment. Such extensive calculations fall well outside the scope of this report. However, Table 4.17 provides a crude measure of force size credibility for deterrent purposes (initial border defense) based on the MAP countries' current ratios of troops per kilometer of border that conceivably would need to be defended (excluding borders with NATO countries and sea coast). The data are presented as a ratio of troops per kilometer of border with current non-NATO countries and, as an alternative and more telling indicator, as a ratio of troops per kilometer of border with countries that are not in NATO, not MAP, and not in the EU. Table 4.18 presents the same information for the non-NATO EU countries. For comparative purposes, Table 4.19 then presents the same data for current NATO members that are on NATO's exterior border—i.e., that border countries that are non-NATO, non-MAP, and non-EU. This list includes only four states (for purposes of this categorization, Switzerland is treated as an EU country).

Although it is an extremely crude indicator, the ratio of troops per potentially defendable border does illustrate the wide variance and different patterns among aspiring members. If we assume that NATO's minimum acceptable threshold for troops per kilometer of defendable border is equal to the lowest such ratio of a current NATO

Table 4.17

Troops and Border Length Ratios: MAP States

State	Peacetime Active Force Size, 2000[a]	Total Land Border + Coastline (km)	Border with Current Non-NATO States (km)	Troops/km of Current Non-NATO Border	Border with Non-NATO, Non-MAP, Non-EU (km)	Troops/km of Non-NATO, Non-MAP, Non-EU Border
Albania	47,000	720 + 362	438	107	287	164
Bulgaria	79,760	1,808 + 354	1,074	74	318	251
Estonia	4,800	633 + 3,794	633	8	294	16
Latvia	5,050	1,150 + 531	1,150	4	358	14
Lithuania	12,700	1,273 + 99	1,182	11	729	17
Macedonia	16,000	748 + 0	520	31	221	72
Romania	207,000	2,508 + 225	2,065	100	1,457	142
Slovakia	38,600	1,355 + 0	181	213	90	429
Slovenia	9,000	1,334 + 47	1,000	9	670	13

NOTE: Border lengths from *The World Factbook 2000*; http://www.odci.gov/cia/publications/factbook/index.html.

[a]Data from IISS, *The Military Balance, 2000–2001*.

Table 4.18

Troops and Border Length Ratios: Non-NATO EU States

State	Peacetime Active Force Size, 2000[a]	Total Land Border + Coastline (km)	Border with Current Non-NATO States (km)	Troops/km of Current Non-NATO Border	Border with Non-NATO, Non-MAP, Non-EU (km)[b]	Troops/km of Non-NATO, Non-MAP, Non-EU Border
Austria	35,500	2,562 + 0	620	57	0	N/A
Finland	31,700	2,628 + 1,126	1,899	17	1,313	24
Sweden	52,700	2,205 + 3,218	586	90	0	N/A

NOTE: Border lengths from *The World Factbook 2000*; http://www.odci.gov/cia/publications/factbook/index.html.

[a]Data from IISS, *The Military Balance, 2000–2001*.

[b]For purposes of border calculations, Switzerland and Liechtenstein are treated as EU countries.

Table 4.19

Troops and Border Length Ratios: "Exterior" NATO Members

State	Peacetime Active Force Size, 2000[a]	Total Land Border + Coastline (km)	Border with Current Non-NATO States (km)	Troops/km of Current Non-NATO Border	Border with Non-NATO, Non-MAP, Non-EU (km)	Troops/km of Non-NATO, Non-MAP, Non-EU Border
Hungary	43,790	2,009 + 0	2,009	22	583	75
Norway	26,700	2,515 + 21,925	2,515	11	167	160
Poland	217,290	2,888 + 491	1,774	122	1,239	175
Turkey	609,700	2,627 + 7,200	2,421	252	2,181	280

NOTE: Border lengths from *The World Factbook 2000*; http://www.odci.gov/cia/publications/factbook/index.html.

[a]Data from IISS, *The Military Balance, 2000–2001.*

member, then Hungary's ratio of 75 troops per kilometer of defendable border establishes the rough standard. And because this measure does not take into account a multitude of important factors, we must assume that the figure may vary by up to 33 percent, depending on the local situation. The result is a figure of 50 troops per kilometer as a rough approximation of a credible border defense.

Based on this calculation, four aspiring members—Estonia, Latvia, Lithuania, and Slovenia—fall so far below the threshold (all having ratios of 13 to 17 troops per kilometer) as to raise questions about the credibility of their deterrent. Perhaps the small covering force suffices because of a perceived lack of a military threat, and in the case of Slovenia, the higher technological sophistication of its forces probably offsets some of the low coverage. However, should a threat develop, the forces of these four countries may be insufficient for deterrence and initial defense. On the other hand, the calculations show a high level of over-preparation on the part of some of the aspiring countries. Slovakia's force size is extremely high when expressed in terms of troops per defendable border. Bulgarian force size is also on the high side, with Albania, Romania, and Macedonia falling within the normal range.

All other things being equal and under conditions of no surprises, NATO is likely to prefer countries that can provide for their own initial border defense. Otherwise, it could have to station troops in these countries to provide even a minimum deterrent. Thus, based on force sizes remaining similar to their present situation, the accessions of Estonia, Latvia, Lithuania, and possibly Slovenia are likely to entail more costs than benefits. On the other hand, the high over-preparation of Slovakia and Bulgaria, especially in view of their low per-troop defense expenditure ratios, means that these two countries need to go through a military reform process that leads to modern and smaller forces. Without such reform, Slovakia and Bulgaria offer a suboptimal force size. These forces would not entail costs in terms of NATO's having to provide a credible deterrent, but they are not as modern as they could be, so substantial opportunity costs become an issue.

Composite Assessment of Strategic Position

Based on the analyses performed so far, an overall assessment can be made of new members' utility to NATO. In terms of strategic position, the overall scale is designed to take into account the aspiring country's attractiveness to NATO with respect to all four criteria:

1. The ability to project power in areas of likely contingencies

2. The creation of interior and defensible borders

3. Risks due to new commitments

4. Added transaction costs

The third, risks category is divided into three subcategories: (1) potential for becoming drawn into bilateral disputes, (2) opportunity costs stemming from the need to make commitment real, and (3) negative impact on overall security situation. Based on the discussion so far, each of the recognized aspirants is assessed along each dimension in a binary fashion, with its attractiveness to NATO coded as high and its lack of attractiveness to NATO coded as low. Each of the categories is assumed to be equal in importance. In the "new risks" category, each of the three categories is taken into account and scored individually, and a composite score for that category is then noted. For "power projection," a location that would assist with NATO's operations in the Balkans is coded as high, while a location that would not greatly alter NATO's Balkan operations is coded as low. For "interior borders," a high grade means that an individual admission would lower the costs to NATO of residual collective defense responsibilities. In terms of "new risks," the potential presence of bilateral disputes is coded as low (because of the low attractiveness to NATO); its absence is coded as high. Regarding opportunity costs, current efforts to upgrade infrastructures in aspiring member states on or near the Balkan peninsula mean a score of high for these states. The aspiring members elsewhere would entail opportunity costs in relation to the current NATO focus on the Balkans; they thus are scored as low (for low attractiveness to NATO). In terms of overall impact on the security environment, countries bordering on Russia are coded as low (for low attractiveness to NATO). For "transaction costs," a high level of preparation for the EU (and potential for membership in this decade) means a high score (for high attractiveness and low added transaction costs).

An overall score is derived based on a score of 1 for high and 0 for low for each of the previous four categories. The composite score in the third category is based on each subcategory score amounting to 0.33, for a total that may range from 0 to 1. The overall score, which can range from 0 to 4, presents a rough measure of where the various aspiring countries stand vis-à-vis NATO in terms of their attractiveness and potential to improve NATO's strategic position. The higher the score, the more attractive the state. Table 4.20 presents the results, which show that Slovakia and Slovenia received the highest score (4) for strategic position. Table 4.21 presents the same assessment for three EU members not in NATO.

Composite Assessment of Military Forces

A similar exercise aimed at quantifying the earlier analyses provides an overall assessment of the armed forces of the aspiring members, taking into account the two criteria:

1. Ability to contribute to power projection missions

2. Sufficiency for deterrence and border defense

Table 4.20

Assessment of Strategic Position: MAP States

State	Power Projection	Interior Borders	New Risks	Transaction Costs	Overall[a]
Albania	High (1)	Low (0)	Mid-high (LHH) (0.7)	Low (0)	Medium (1.7)
Bulgaria	High (1)	Low (0)	High (HHH) (1.0)	Low (0)	Medium (2)
Estonia	Low (0)	Low (0)	Low (LLL) (0.0)	High (1)	Low (1)
Latvia	Low (0)	Low (0)	Low (LLL) (0.0)	High (1)	Low (1)
Lithuania	Low (0)	Low (0)	Mid-low (HLL) (0.3)	High (1)	Low (1.3)
Macedonia	High (1)	Low (0)	Mid-high (LHH) (0.7)	Low (0)	Medium (1.7)
Romania	High (1)	Low (0)	High (HHH) (1.0)	Low (0)	Medium (2)
Slovakia	High (1)	High (1)	High (HHH) (1.0)	High (1)	High (4)
Slovenia	High (1)	High (1)	High (HHH) (1.0)	High (1)	High (4)

NOTE: For each of the four categories, high = 1, low = 0.

[a]Overall score ranged from a minimum of 0 to a maximum of 4; the resulting 5-point scale was divided into three sections, with the middle section being the largest (distribution is 1.5, 2.0, 1.5). The three sections were coded in the following manner: 0–1.5 = low; 1.6–3.5 = medium; 3.6–5 = high.

Table 4.21

Assessment of Strategic Position: Non-NATO EU Members

State	Power Projection	Interior Borders	New Risks	Transaction Costs	Overall[a]
Austria	High (1)	High (1)	Mid-high (HHH) (1.0)	High (1)	High (4)
Finland	Low (0)	Low (0)	Mid-low (HLL) (0.3)	High (1)	Low (1.3)
Sweden	Low (0)	Low (0)	Mid-high (HLH) (0.7)	High (1)	Medium (1.7)

NOTE: For each of the four categories, high = 1, low = 0.

[a]Overall score ranged from a minimum of 0 to a maximum of 4; the resulting 5-point scale was divided into three sections, with the middle section being the largest (distribution is 1.5, 2.0, 1.5). The three sections were coded in the following manner: 0–1.5 = low; 1.6–3.5 = medium; 3.6–5 = high.

Based on the earlier discussion, each of the recognized aspirants is assessed along each dimension, in a binary fashion, with its attractiveness to NATO coded as high, and its lack of attractiveness to NATO coded as low. Each of the categories is assumed to be equal in importance. In the "power projection" category, countries are coded on a scale of 1 to 4, with 1 being the least attractive and 4 being the most (see matrix, Figure 4.1). Large and more-modern forces are assumed to be the most attractive and are given a high score of 4 points. The next highest category comprises countries having small but more-modern armed forces and countries having large and less-modern (though not rated "very low" on the modernization scale) armed forces; these are given a medium-high score of 3. The next category includes countries in the small and less-modern category but not in the very-low classification; these are given a medium-low score of 2. The least-attractive countries, from the viewpoint of NATO power projection missions, are those whose forces are rated as very low on the modernization scale; these are given a score of 1. For the "deterence" category, the ability to provide a deterrent without NATO reinforcement is assumed to make a state attractive. Countries are coded on a scale of 1 to 4, with 1 as the least attractive and 4 as the most. The coding is in relation to the current NATO "floor" level of 75 (Hungary) for troops per kilometer of non-NATO, non-MAP, non-EU border (see Tables 4.17 and 4.19). Countries with forces equal to or greater than the current NATO "floor" level (75 or more) are coded as high; those with forces 33 percent less than the "floor" level (50 to 74) are coded as medium-high; those with forces 33 to 66 percent less than the "floor" level (25 to 49) are coded as medium-low; and those with forces less than 25 percent of the "floor" level (24 or less) are coded as low. An overall score is then derived based on a combined score for each of the two categories. This overall score presents a rough measure of where the various aspiring members stand vis-à-vis NATO in terms of their armed forces' attractiveness. Table 4.22 presents the results. Of the MAP states, Slovakia received the highest score and the only overall score of high. Albania, Bulgaria, Macedonia, and Romania received medium scores, as did Estonia and Slovenia, though these latter two were a bit lower than the others in this group. Latvia and Lithuania followed, with low scores. Table 4.23 presents the same assessment for three EU members currently not in NATO.

Composite Assessment of Strategic Rationale

Finally, the overall scores from both categories, strategic position and armed forces, are combined to produce a complete picture of each aspiring member's strategic attractiveness to NATO. The two categories are assumed to be equal in importance. Because the two assessments use different scales, the earlier scores are standardized on a 0–10 scale (in other words, the overall scores from Tables 4.20 and 4.22 are converted to the same scale so as to derive an overall

Table 4.22

Assessment of Armed Forces: MAP States

State	Power Projection	Deterrence	Overall[a]
Albania	Low (1)	High (4)	Medium (5)
Bulgaria	Low (1)	High (4)	Medium (5)
Estonia	Medium-high (3)	Low (1)	Medium (4)
Latvia	Medium-low (2)	Low (1)	Low (3)
Lithuania	Medium-low (2)	Low (1)	Low (3)
Macedonia	Medium-low (2)	Medium-high (3)	Medium (5)
Romania	Low (1)	High (4)	Medium (5)
Slovakia	Medium-high (3)	High (4)	High (7)
Slovenia	Medium-high (3)	Low (1)	Medium (4)

NOTE: For the two categories, high = 4, low = 1.
[a]Overall score ranged from a minimum of 2 to a maximum of 8; the resulting 7-point scale was divided into three sections, with the middle section being the largest (distribution is 2,3,2). The three sections were coded in the following manner: 2–3 = low; 4–6 = medium; 7–8 = high.

Table 4.23

Assessment of Armed Forces: Non-NATO EU Members

State	Power Projection	Deterrence	Overall[a]
Austria	High (4)	High (4)	High (8)
Finland	High (4)	Low (1)	Medium (5)
Sweden	High (4)	High (4)	High (8)

NOTE: For the two categories, high = 4, low = 1.
[a]Overall score ranged from a minimum of 2 to a maximum of 8; the resulting 7-point scale was divided into three sections, with the middle section being the largest (distribution is 2,3,2). The three sections were coded in the following manner: 2–3 = low; 4–6 = medium; 7–8 = high.

and non-biased score for the two categories). The overall score presents a rough measure of where the various countries stand vis-à-vis NATO in terms of their attractiveness, based on a strategic rationale and a cost-benefit assessment of what their membership would mean for NATO. Table 4.24 presents the results, showing that Slovakia received the highest overall score. Table 4.25 presents the same assessment for three EU members currently not in NATO.

Table 4.24

Assessment of Strategic Attractiveness: MAP States

State	Strategic Position	Armed Forces	Overall Assessment[a]
Albania	4.2	5.0	3.6 (Medium)
Bulgaria	5.0	5.0	5.0 (Medium)
Estonia	2.5	3.3	2.9 (Low)
Latvia	2.5	1.7	2.1 (Low)
Lithuania	3.3	1.7	2.5 (Low)
Macedonia	4.2	5.0	4.6 (Medium)
Romania	5.0	5.0	5.0 (Medium)
Slovakia	10.0	8.3	9.2 (High)
Slovenia	10.0	3.3	6.7 (Medium)

NOTE: Overall scores from Tables 4.20 and 4.22 converted to a 0–10 scale. For example, Albania's 1.7 overall score on strategic position (Table 4.20), based on a 0–4 scale, translates into 4.2 on a 0–10 scale. Albania's 5.0 overall score on armed forces (Table 4.22), based on a 2–8 scale, translates into 5.0 on a 0–10 scale.

[a]Overall score is a median of the scores in the two previous columns. Overall score ranged from a minimum of 0 to a maximum of 10; the resulting 11-point scale was divided into three sections, with the middle section being the largest (distribution is 30%, 40%, 30%). The overall section was coded in the following manner: 0–3 = low; 3.1–6.9 = medium; 7–10 = high.

Table 4.25

Assessment of Strategic Attractiveness: Non-NATO EU Members

State	Strategic Position	Armed Forces	Overall Assessment[a]
Austria	10.0	10.0	10.0 (High)
Finland	3.3	5.0	4.2 (Medium)
Sweden	4.2	10.0	7.1 (High)

NOTE: Overall scores from Tables 4.21 and 4.23 converted to a 0–10 scale. For example, Finland's 1.3 overall score on strategic position (Table 4.21), based on a 0–4 scale, translates into 3.3 on a 0–10 scale. Finland's 5.0 overall score on armed forces (Table 4.23), based on a 2–8 scale, translates into 5.0 on a 0–10 scale.

[a]Overall score is a median of the scores in the two previous columns. Overall score ranged from a minimum of 0 to a maximum of 10; the resulting 11-point scale was divided into three sections, with the middle section being the largest (distribution is 30%, 40%, 30%). The overall section was coded in the following manner: 0–3 = low; 3.1–6.9 = medium; 7–10 = high.

The results in Table 4.24 indicate that, from the perspective of strategic rationale, the aspiring members fall into three groups, as follows:

- Slovakia is highly attractive to NATO.

- Slovenia, Bulgaria, Romania, Macedonia, and Albania (in that order) form a middle group that is of some attractiveness to NATO.

- Estonia, Lithuania, and Latvia (in that order) are of low attractiveness to NATO.

If the results for the EU members not in NATO (Table 4.25) are included in the calculations, Austria is the most attractive potential NATO member, based solely on the strategic criteria outlined above. Sweden is also attractive to NATO, and Finland is less so.

FINAL ASSESSMENT

Combination of each country's overall scores on its ability to meet NATO's pre-conditions and its strategic attractiveness to NATO results in a final assessment of each potential member's preparation for and attractiveness to NATO. Figure 4.2 summarizes the data arrived at earlier on the preparation and attractiveness of the MAP and non-NATO EU countries for NATO membership.

Table 4.26 presents the same information in a numerical format for the aspiring NATO members, and Table 4.27 does the same for the three EU members not in NATO. Figure 4.3 presents the combined results in graph format.

Using the methodology presented here and the assessments derived from it, the following conclusions can be drawn regarding the "long list" of potential NATO members:

- Of the MAP states, Slovenia is the most qualified and attractive candidate for membership from NATO's strategic perspective. The costs of Slovene integration will be virtually nil, and the benefits, though small, will be potentially significant in view of NATO's focus on the Balkans.

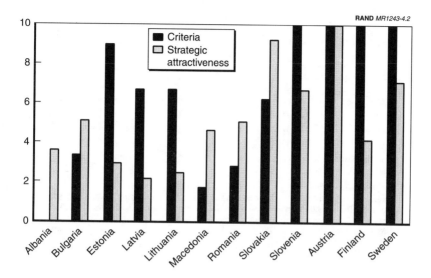

SOURCE: Overall assessments in Tables 4.16, 4.24, and 4.25.

Figure 4.2—Overall Assessment of Extent to Which Countries Meet NATO Criteria and Countries' Strategic Attractiveness: MAP States and Non-NATO EU Members

Table 4.26

Assessment of Preparation for and Attractiveness to NATO: MAP States

State	Criteria[a]	Strategic Attractiveness[b]	Overall[c]
Albania	Low (0.0)	Medium (3.6)	Low (1.8)
Bulgaria	Medium (3.3)	Medium (5.0)	Medium (4.2)
Estonia	High (8.9)	Low (2.9)	Medium (5.9)
Latvia	Medium (6.7)	Low (2.1)	Medium (4.4)
Lithuania	Medium (6.7)	Low (2.5)	Medium (4.6)
Macedonia	Low (1.7)	Medium (4.6)	Medium-low (3.2)
Romania	Low (2.8)	Medium (5.0)	Medium-low (3.9)
Slovakia	Medium (6.2)	High (9.2)	Medium-high (7.7)
Slovenia	High (10.0)	Medium (6.7)	High (8.4)

[a]Data from Table 4.16.

[b]Data from Table 4.24.

[c]Overall score is a median of the scores in the two previous columns. Overall score ranged from a minimum of 0 to a maximum of 10; the resulting 11-point scale was divided into five categories: low, medium-low, medium, medium-high, high (equal distribution). Thus, 0–2.0 = low; 2.1–4.0 = medium-low; 4.1–6.0 = medium; 6.1–8.0 = medium-high; 8.1–10 = high.

Table 4.27

Assessment of Preparation for and Attractiveness to NATO: Non-NATO EU Members

State	Criteria[a]	Strategic Attractiveness[b]	Overall[c]
Austria	High (10.0)	High (10.0)	High (10.0)
Finland	High (10.0)	Medium (4.2)	Medium-high (7.1)
Sweden	High (10.0)	High (7.1)	High (8.6)

[a]Criteria assumed to be fully met, based on current membership in the EU and high Freedom House ratings (Table 4.12).

[b]Data from Table 4.25.

[c]Overall score is a median of the scores in the two previous columns. Overall score ranged from a minimum of 0 to a maximum of 10; the resulting 11-point scale was divided into five categories: low, medium-low, medium, medium-high, high (equal distribution). Thus, 0–2.0 = low; 2.1–4.0 = medium–low; 4.1–6.0 = medium; 6.1–8.0 = medium-high; 8.1–10 = high.

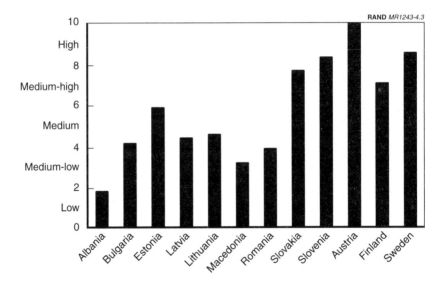

SOURCE: Overall assessments in Tables 4.26 and 4.27.

Figure 4.3—Final Combined Assessment of Preparation for and Attractiveness to NATO: MAP States

- Slovakia is next in line. Its slightly lower overall attractiveness compared with Slovenia is mitigated by its relatively larger and more-modern armed forces. Slovakia straddles the northern and southern axis of NATO's enlargement; the costs of its integration will be low, and the benefits will be modest but visible.

- Estonia, Lithuania, and Latvia are mid-term (or longer) candidates. Their advanced stage in meeting NATO's criteria is offset by the strategic ramifications of their accession.

- Bulgaria and Romania follow. Their relative strategic attractiveness is offset by their inability to meet NATO's criteria.

- Macedonia and especially Albania are the least advanced in meeting NATO's criteria. Their prospects for membership are distinctly long-term, and current activities center on their evolving into real candidates.

- Of the EU members currently not in NATO, Austria is in a good position to join if it chooses to do so. To a lesser extent, so is Sweden. Finnish membership, however, would entail some difficulties because of the strategic costs it would impose on NATO.

Of course, the positions just described are in no way permanent. The assessments assume a continuing evolution along the currently followed path. If, for instance, Slovenia were to substantially diverge from its path by, say, slashing its defense budget radically, its chances for NATO membership would be negatively affected. Similarly, if Slovakia's democratic coalition were to unravel and Slovakia returned to the more-authoritarian norms associated with the pre-October 1998 Meciar-led coalition, its chances for NATO membership would suffer accordingly. But changes can also go in a positive direction. If, for example, Romania manages to push through a far-reaching military reform program and makes substantial progress in meeting NATO's political and economic criteria, its membership chances will improve.

The reasoning behind the categorization used here is also subject to change if an unexpected and especially exogenously influenced shift in the security environment occurs. Conceivably, and depending on the specific causes of the shift, enlargement could take on a much faster pace and proceed with highly relaxed accession criteria.

The seeming dichotomy between NATO's pronouncements about an "open door" (as stipulated in NATO's founding document) and its current highly selective way of choosing new members has provoked complaints among some of the MAP countries. The most strenuous objections have come from Lithuania, Latvia, and Estonia, whose officials have asked NATO to admit openly that strategic criteria not contained in NATO's 1995 enlargement study are nonetheless ever-present, curtailing their chances of ever becoming members.

These objections have some validity, but they miss the point. As long as NATO retains aspects of a military alliance, it cannot be expected to forgo strategic criteria in its decisions to extend security guarantees. For its own reasons of wishing to keep complete control of the enlargement process, NATO has refused to be locked into making enlargement decisions solely on the basis of whether or not aspiring members meet the pre-conditions set for them. Moreover, the seeming incompatibility between NATO's pronouncements and its deeds serves the overall cause of European security, even for countries such as Estonia, Latvia, and Lithuania. NATO faces a complex situation. It does not want to rupture its relations with Russia by proceeding to invite Estonia, Latvia, and Lithuania into the alliance, but it also does not want to allow Russia to intimidate the three states. By placing Estonia, Latvia, and Lithuania on a path to eventual membership, NATO has elevated its commitment to them and clearly indicated that it sees their sovereignty as a strategic asset. The lack of clarity in NATO's security guarantee to these three states serves the purposes of deterrence by indicating that NATO would impose far-reaching costs on Russia for any encroachment on their sovereignty. At the same time, the security guarantee stops short of putting NATO's relationship with Russia at risk by refusing to specify dates for these states' accession. As one analyst noted:

> Russian actions which violate reasonable norms require the appropriate criticism and condemnation by the rest of the international community. It is, however, in the West's direct self-interest to promote a more constructive Russian posture in European security affairs.[23]

---

[23]Roland Danreuther, "Escaping the Enlargement Trap in NATO-Russian Relations," *Survival*, 41:4, Winter 1999–2000, p. 161.

Taking into account the Russian objections to NATO's enlargement in the eastern Baltic littoral does not necessarily mean accepting the validity of those objections. But it does mean making a careful cost-benefit assessment that includes an evaluation of the effect that a less-constructive Russian posture will have on overall European security. Conceivably, Estonia, Latvia, and Lithuania could be in their current stage well into the next decade. The low chances of their joining NATO in the near- or even mid-term under conditions of continuance of current security trends do not mean, however, that NATO has no stake or interest in their continuing sovereignty. Somewhat paradoxically, NATO has a special interest in these three countries and in defense cooperation with them because of their strategic situation. However, NATO membership for these countries is not around the corner.

The assessments provided here are not policy recommendations as to which members should or should not be invited into NATO. Instead, they are a necessary first step for thinking about both a long-term shaping strategy for the MAP countries and the specific activities that the strategy may entail for NATO, EUCOM, and USAFE. As one analyst noted, "[Predicting] which countries NATO will invite to join in 2002 is an uncertain but important business—important, because the alliance should be prepared for the consequences."[24] The purpose of the methodology presented here is to discern the most likely course of action NATO might take regarding enlargement in the next 10 to 15 years based on a series of clearly defined assumptions about NATO's evolution, the explicit criteria NATO has established for considering future members, and the implicit considerations that guide any major foreign policy move.

Within the constraints of the main assumption that current security trends will continue, what emerges as the most likely path for NATO enlargement is as follows. NATO's enlargement is likely to continue, because the process establishes the foundation not only for NATO's post–Cold War relevance, but for NATO's imposition of a behavioral regime in the unintegrated part of Europe, which has been instrumental in creating the current benign security regime. Future en-

---

[24]Michael Mihalka, "Enlargement Deferred: More Political Instability for Romania? A Rejoinder," *Security Dialogue*, 30:4, December 1999, pp. 497–502.

largement is likely to proceed at a slower pace than previously, how-ever, with fewer countries invited to become members. One to four states might join in the 2000–10 decade, with perhaps another one or two in the five years following. Of the MAP countries, Slovenia and Slovakia are the most likely to be the earliest entrants. Projections beyond these two clear choices are murky, however, and because other MAP countries are candidates in the mid- or long-term, are subject to considerable uncertainty based on the countries' internal evolution. Because of the strategic problems their accession poses, Lithuania, Latvia, and Estonia are likely to remain in their current MAP position for a considerable period of time, perhaps joining the EU first so as to strengthen the extent of their "soft" security guaran-tee from NATO. Of the current EU members that are not NATO members, Austria, if it decided to seek membership, would be an attractive candidate for NATO, followed by Sweden.

The next chapter follows up on this analysis by examining the mili-tary implications of the enlargement process and the shaping priori-ties that emerge for the U.S. armed forces.

Chapter Five

SHAPING THE FORCES OF ASPIRING MEMBERS

The current status of military reform in the MAP countries largely determines the nature of shaping policies and the form of military cooperation established with their armed forces. Whether a MAP state is attempting to finalize its readiness for operations in a NATO framework or to set up a minimum credible deterrent, the current status and future direction of its military have profound implications for NATO defense planning. All MAP states face challenges in attempting to reshape their military forces, and certain states face particularly significant problems. These issues are the subject of this chapter, which assesses the status of military reform in each of the countries aspiring to NATO membership in order to identify shaping priorities in U.S. defense planning.

The analysis begins by assessing the general characteristics of the armed forces of the aspiring countries. Table 5.1 presents these characteristics for the current and future armed forces of the nine MAP states, broken down by service.

As the tables make clear, the limited manpower and general low technological sophistication and readiness levels of the individual MAP states mean that these countries have the potential to make only a minor (though not irrelevant) military contribution to NATO's collective defense and power projection missions over the next 10 to 15 years. For the foreseeable future, these militaries will remain dominated by ground forces, and these countries' defense budgets (except Slovenia's) will continue to be much smaller (in an absolute sense) than those of current NATO members of similar size.

Table 5.1

Armed Forces, by Services: MAP States

State	Peace-time Active Force Size, 2000[a]	Planned Active Force Size, 2004[b]	Defense Expenditures/ Troop, 1999– 2000 (in US$)[a]	2000 Army Peacetime (% of total force size)[c]	2000 Navy Peacetime (% of total force size)[c]	2000 Air Force Peacetime (% of total force size)[c]
Albania	47,000	?	681	40,000 (85.1%)	2,500 (5.3%)	4,500 (9.6%)
Bulgaria	79,760	50,000	3,573	42,400 (53.2%)	5,260 (6.6%)	18,300 (22.9%)
Estonia	4,800	~7,000[d]	11,875	4,320 (90.0%)	250 (5.2%)	140 (2.9%)
Latvia	5,050	~8,000[d]	9,109	2,400 (47.5%)	840 (16.6%)	210 (4.2%)
Lithuania	12,700	~15,000[d]	9,764	9,340 (73.5%)	560 (4.4%)	800 (6.3%)
Macedonia	16,000	~20,000	7,313	15,000 (93.8%)	N/A	700 (4.3%)
Romania	207,000	112,000	2,614	106,000 (51.2%)	20,800 (10.0%)	43,500 (21.0%)
Slovakia	38,600	30,000	9,119	23,800 (65.0%)	N/A	11,500 (29.8%)
Slovenia	9,000	~9,000	38,333	8,780 (97.6%)	100[e] (1.1%)	120[e] (1.3%)

[a]Data from Table 4.6.

[b]Data from various ministries of defense and national news sources. Where a reform plan is in place, the actual figure is given; where a reform plan is under discussion, an approximate number is provided.

[c]Data from IISS, *The Military Balance, 2000–2001.* Percentages may not add up to 100 because of central, headquarters, and other troops not included in the service totals.

[d]Estonian, Latvian, and Lithuanian forces will be highly integrated as part of Baltic cooperation.

[e]Slovenia's air and naval elements are part of its army.

In general, their most valuable contributions to NATO missions will come from their ground forces. In terms of relevant air force contributions, the MAP states will have little more than token forces to offer (and sometimes not even that). In the short- and mid-term, the most important benefit to be gained by NATO and USAF from the enlargement process could be NATO's unconstrained access to and use of the aspiring members' infrastructure and airspace. In other words, their limited military capabilities notwithstanding, the new and aspiring members will provide geostrategic depth to NATO, making NATO's power projection mission easier in and around Europe.

OVERALL CHALLENGES

The MAP states face many challenges in attempting to reform their militaries. Their military establishments show the legacy of the communist-style model (with its emphasis on ground-forces-dominant, mass-based, and heavy forces) in their training, doctrine, and equipment and in the fact that their officer corps was accustomed to resources being prioritized for defense and the military being autonomous from civilian political leaders. Because of this legacy, the quality of the MAP countries' contribution to NATO operations hinges on a number of factors, including the effectiveness and pace of asset modernization; improvements in training and readiness; adjustment to NATO's doctrine, tactics, and procedures; and the initiation of planning under conditions of civilian control of the militaries and serious constraints on resources. Most of all, a given MAP state's optimal contribution to NATO implies adoption of planning techniques that integrate resource availability with strategies and needs (an integrated planning, programming, and budgeting system akin to the U.S. PPBS is one example).

With a well-thought-out plan of development, wise investments in modernization, and increased operations and maintenance (O&M) spending, the armed forces of the MAP states eventually could make a meaningful, if small, military contribution. NATO can help shape the choices the aspiring members make in their plans, though NATO's preferences may not always be the same as those of the aspiring members. How the two are reconciled is of significant interest to NATO from the standpoint of future operations in and around Europe.

Use of Resources

Theoretically, and purely from NATO's perspective, the MAP states should use their resources to provide NATO with forces that promote maximum efficiency at the alliance level. Since efficiency in this case entails a measure of specialization in order to build on NATO's current assets and take advantage of potential members' comparative advantages, the MAP states stand to contribute more to NATO if, instead of building up their forces across the board, they emphasize specific branches of service, build on existing strengths, and focus on the prospective missions their armed forces might undertake.

Generally, optimal efficiency within an alliance is not achievable, because alliances are not all that efficient in providing military forces—there is much duplication and inefficiency in the use of resources. However, NATO is in a unique position to ensure a large measure of efficiency in the MAP states' force development because of its leverage and the incentives the MAP states have to adjust to NATO's preferences. In this sense, the more a MAP state wants to join NATO, the more it can be expected to adjust to NATO's preferences for force development. To cite one example, Estonia's perceived dependence on NATO to safeguard its long-term security means that Estonia is likely to follow NATO's advice in developing its military.

These incentives diminish for a MAP state once it is invited to join NATO. At that stage, and especially after the country becomes a NATO member, NATO's formal means for shaping its force development are limited to such mechanisms as target force goals[1] and coordination of defense policies, supplemented by a variety of informal mechanisms and bilateral and multilateral fora. Although informative, these mechanisms cannot force a member to subordinate its own preferences in defense policy to what would be best from NATO's perspective, as befits a democratically based alliance such as NATO. Indeed, establishment of the MAP mechanism shows an understanding of such an incentive structure (as well as lessons learned from the initial 1997–99 round of enlargement), since MAP's military aim is to effect changes in each state's armed forces prior to its accession.[2] None of what has been said here should be interpreted to mean that NATO should take a domineering course of ac-

---

[1] For more on the mechanics of NATO's force planning process, see Frank Boland (Head, Force Planning Section of NATO's Defense Planning and Operations Division), *NATO Review*, 46:3, Autumn 1998, pp. 32–35 (http://www.nato.int/docu/review/1998/9803-09.htm).

[2] MAP, with its bilateral meetings, consultations, and feedback to the defense officials of the MAP states, approximates NATO's target force goal process but includes real incentives for the given states to meet NATO's recommendations.

tion vis-à-vis the MAP states. What it does mean is that NATO has the means to shape defense planning in the MAP states by advancing real reform that, in the end, is beneficial to both the MAP state and NATO.

Individual country choices in the aspiring states are likely to emphasize domestic considerations at the expense of NATO's needs. Thus, from NATO's perspective, country choices are likely to yield a less efficient use of resources, driven by factors such as prestige, economic motives (desire to keep a semblance of an industrial base in place in specific areas), pork-barrel democratic politics, or incompletely developed planning and procurement MoD processes. But the end result may be that each MAP state attempts to embark on a costly modernization program that could result in a highly inefficient outcome. In this sense, NATO's preferences will amount to countervailing tendencies regarding the preferences that result solely from the aspiring member's decisionmaking processes. It is in this sense that the enlargement process can assist aspiring members in building a more effective military establishment for deterrence purposes, contributing more efficiently to NATO's missions, and implementing an efficient resource management and planning system to free up resources for non-military parts of state budgets.

Besides maximizing NATO's gains, greater efficiency in defense spending is optimal for all concerned. Greater specialization emphasizing ground forces produces an enhanced deterrent in that it provides prospective members with stronger ground defense capabilities and a consequent lower likelihood that NATO will be called on to provide assistance and reinforcement. In addition, aspiring members gain because their contribution to NATO is more valuable and their role in NATO and their security are enhanced.

"Oversized" and "Emerging" MAP Armed Forces

An examination of the armed forces of the MAP states reveals two common patterns: oversized militaries and emerging militaries. The first pattern fits MAP countries that were states prior to 1989 (Bulgaria, Romania, and Albania) or that inherited a largely intact armed forces from a former state (Slovakia) and have continued to field armed forces larger (in terms of structure, manpower, and equipment) than the armed forces of NATO countries of similar size.

These "oversized" armed forces have had to adjust to far-reaching cuts in defense budgets and a redirection of resources away from them and toward their countries' transitioning economies, which means that their quality has suffered. Because most of the remaining defense budget goes to support the still extensive personnel structure, these countries have cut back on O&M allocations and have reduced procurement to almost negligible levels. Lack of funds for spare parts and maintenance has led to large quantities of nonoperational equipment. As a result, these militaries tend to be of mediocre quality, with shortcomings in training and a larger share of obsolescent or obsolete equipment than is found in the militaries of comparable-size NATO countries. Moreover, these problems are magnified in technology-intensive services, such as the air force.[3]

This group of MAP countries with oversized militaries has problems similar to those faced by new members Poland, Hungary, and the Czech Republic, though the oversized MAP militaries tend to have more obsolete equipment and larger training and readiness problems. Of these MAP countries, Slovakia has the most-modern equipment, on a par with that of Poland and the Czech Republic, and Bulgaria and Romania come next. Albania has equipment that is not only obsolete (World War II or Korean War vintage) but mostly nonfunctioning; indeed, the Albanian state itself has not recovered fully from its collapse in 1997.

The second pattern, that of emerging militaries, fits the MAP states that gained their sovereignty in the early 1990s (Estonia, Latvia, Lithuania, Macedonia, and Slovenia) and have had to build their armed forces essentially from scratch. These "emerging" militaries exhibit basic problems—lack of equipment and lack of trained personnel. Among them, Slovenia fields the best forces (because of its relative wealth), and Estonia, Latvia, and Lithuania follow. Macedonia's armed forces are still at an early stage of development.

---

[3]For a succinct overview of the problems facing the militaries of the former communist states, see Christopher Donnelly, "Defense Transformation in the New Democracies," *NATO Review*, 44:6, November 1996, pp. 20–23 (http://www.nato.int/docu/review/articles/9606-5.htm).

CHALLENGES RELATED TO AIR FORCES

The ongoing integration of Poland, the Czech Republic, and Hungary into NATO offers lessons for the integration of the MAP states. The experience so far shows that, arguably, one of the most difficult problems facing the new members is modernization of their air forces. The large costs of modern combat aircraft, the limited utility of existing Soviet-made air assets for NATO operations, the generally limited defense resources, and the multiple priorities—all of these, together, prevent the new members' air forces from being able to take a meaningful part in NATO air operations. The problem is apparent in the divergence between the progress in interoperability and the significant (brigade-size) forces that each new member has assigned to NATO's land Rapid Reaction Forces (RRF LAND) and the corresponding slower progress and low assignment of air units to NATO.[4] This divergence is also illustrated by the three new members' participation in NATO's peace operations in the Balkans. Each of the three contributed a battalion of either light infantry or engineers to NATO's IFOR/SFOR operation in Bosnia-Herzegovina, made ground troops available for the potentially intensive operations in Kosovo, and contributed units (up to battalion size) to NATO's Operation Joint Guardian in Kosovo. But NATO neither expected nor desired combat air contributions from these new members during Operation Allied Force. The fact that the three most affluent former non-Soviet Warsaw Pact states with the most-modern forces have encountered such problems with air force modernization and integration suggests that the less-modern and poorer MAP states will encounter even more problems. And these problems are multidimensional and defy easy solutions.

Equipment: Combat Aircraft

Whereas the emerging armed forces are in the process of building their air forces and currently possess little equipment of any kind, three of the oversized armed forces—those of Bulgaria, Romania, and Slovakia—have both extensive experience with advanced aircraft and

---

[4]Ian Kemp, "NATO Advances Expansion Aims: Czech, Hungarian and Polish Integration Gathers Momentum," *International Defense Review*, April 2000, pp. 34–40.

small numbers of modern (fourth-generation) combat jet aircraft.[5] These three oversized air forces still show the legacy problems common to former communist countries—large equipment holdings dominated by obsolescent or obsolete airframes whose maintenance has been suspect over the past decade. With improvements in training, modernization of equipment (upgrades to avionics and armament), and a change in operational doctrine, the interceptor and ground support assets of these three aspirants eventually could operate alongside NATO air forces. However, these assets probably would be used only in their home countries, since the extensive costs associated with their operating in NATO's power projection missions seem to exceed both the benefits of and the need for such assets. Table 5.2 presents a general look at the MAP countries' air force inventories. The tables in the Appendix provide more-detailed information about the equipment inventories of the MAP countries.

Table 5.2

Air Force Inventory: MAP States, 2000

State	Advanced Combat Aircraft[a]	Older-Type Combat Aircraft[b]	Armed Jet Trainers[c]	Fixed-Wing Transport (medium)[d]	Combat/Assault Helicopters[e]	Combat Support Helicopters[f]	Light (Utility) Aircraft[g]
Albania		X[h]	X[h]	X[h]			X
Bulgaria	X	X	X	X	X	X	X
Estonia							X
Latvia							X
Lithuania		X	X				X
Macedonia					X		X
Romania	X	X	X	X	X	X	X
Slovakia	X	X	X	X	X	X	X
Slovenia							X

SOURCE: IISS, *Jane's*, Teal Group Corporation, individual ministries of defense (MoDs).
[a]MiG-29.
[b]MiG-23, MiG-21, Su-25, Su-22, IAR-93.
[c]L-39, IAR-99, MiG-15.
[d]An-12, An-24, An-26, C-130.
[e]Mi-24, Mi-8/17, IAR-330, IAR-316.
[f]Mi-8/17.
[g]Includes both fixed- and rotary-wing; may be armed.
[h]Serviceability questionable.

_____

[5]Albania's air force is discussed below, in the section on the emerging militaries.

Since Bulgaria, Romania, and Slovakia have equipment similar to that of the three countries that joined NATO in 1999, the experiences of those newest members in adjusting to NATO are illustrative. Appendix Tables A.1, A.2, and A.3 provide an inventory of aircraft for Bulgaria, Romania, and Slovakia. Poland and Hungary have a small core of modern combat aircraft, MiG-29s (22 and 28, respectively), and all three countries have substantial numbers of obsolete or obsolescent aircraft (MiG-21s, MiG-23s, Su-22s, and Su-25s). By 2004, Poland plans to retain only its MiG-29s and some 60 Su-22s, both types modernized substantially to allow operation in a NATO framework. Hungary will retain only modernized MiG-29s for combat duties. The Czech Republic is procuring a new, indigenously designed light attack jet, an L-159, which will form the mainstay of its air force. For purposes of comparison with the three oversized MAP states, Table 5.3 presents a general look at the inventories of the three members that joined NATO in 1999.

Each of the three new members has expressed interest in procuring NATO-type aircraft as it phases out its obsolete Soviet-built aircraft. At various times, Polish officials have spoken about procurement of 60 to 120 new aircraft, Czech Republic officials about 24 to 36, and

Table 5.3

Air Force Inventory: New (1999) NATO Members, 2000

State	Advanced Combat Aircraft[a]	Older-Type Combat Aircraft[b]	Light Jets/ Armed Trainers[c]	Fixed-Wing Transport (medium)[d]	Combat/ Assault Helicopters[e]	Combat Support Helicopters[f]	Light (Utility) Aircraft[g]
Czech Rep.		X	X	X	X	X	X
Hungary	X	X	X	X	X	X	X
Poland	X	X	X	X	X	X	X

SOURCE: IISS, *Jane's*, Teal Group Corporation, individual MoDs.

[a]MiG-29.

[b]MiG-23, MiG-21, Su-25, Su-22.

[c]L-39, TS-11.

[d]An-24, An-26.

[e]Mi-24, Mi-8/17.

[f]Mi-8/17, W-3.

[g]Includes both fixed- and rotary-wing; may be armed.

[h]Serviceability questionable.

Hungarian officials about 30 to 50. The choices appear to be down to the F-16, the F/A-18, and the JAS-39 *Gripen*.[6] Whether the three new members will manage to find the resources to procure the equipment and the support packages they project and, equally important, whether they will be able to afford the training required to make these weapon systems effective are questions that cannot yet be answered. Currently, it is clear that these countries cannot afford either to purchase or sustain the new aircraft. Indeed, their defense officials began their search for a new fighter aircraft in 1992, but lack of funds, as well as repeated formal and informal urging by NATO and U.S. defense officials to procure more badly needed equipment, led to delays in the decision on the fighter.

In comparison with the three new members, the MAP countries face greater budgetary limitations, which represent the biggest constraint on modernization of their air assets. For example, the cost of 24 new F-16 or F-18 fighter aircraft (one squadron) and the support package is in the vicinity of $1 billion,[7] and this amount does not include armament for the aircraft or the O&M costs necessary to use the aircraft properly. With a slow, multiyear phase-in of such aircraft, and especially if the aircraft were "cascaded" free of charge,[8] Poland probably could make a successful switch to NATO-type combat aircraft in this decade given its relatively large defense budget and assuming it will make further progress in military reform. The Czech Republic and perhaps Hungary (if it can surmount the hurdle of its

---

[6]Since 1993, there has been a great deal of discussion in the three new member countries about procurement of new fighter aircraft. And since 1993–94, Lockheed Martin (F-16), McDonnell Douglas (F-18), and Saab and British Aerospace (*Gripen*) have engaged in intense marketing efforts in the former communist countries in central Europe (see Bjorn Hagelin, "Saab, British Aerospace and the JAS 39 Gripen Aircraft Joint Venture," *European Security*, 7:4, Winter 1998, pp. 91–117).

[7]The unit cost of F-16C/D to the USAF (in FY'98) was $26.9 million; the unit cost of F/A-18C/D to the USAF (in FY'98) was $39.5 million. (Data based on congressional sources compiled at http://www.fas.org/man/dod-101/sys/ac/f-16.htm and http://www.fas.org/man/dod-101/sys/ac/f-18.htm.) The Foreign Military Sale (FMS) of 70 F-16C/D Block 50+ aircraft to Greece in 1999 cost $3.1 billion, meaning a unit cost of $44.3 million. The FMS of 60 F-16C/D Block 50/52 aircraft to Israel in 1998 cost $2.5 billion, meaning a unit cost of $41.7 million.

[8]As NATO members, the three countries that joined in 1999 are eligible for NATO cascading. The United States already has transferred some major excess equipment to the new members (for example, a U.S. Perry-class frigate was transferred to the Polish Navy in March 2000, and another frigate is to follow).

low defense budget) also might be able to do so. But the $1 billion amount far exceeds the total annual defense budget of every one of the nine MAP countries, which means that new supersonic combat aircraft are currently simply beyond their reach. Even if the over-sized MAP air forces (with experience in use of fourth-generation aircraft) were to acquire used F-16 aircraft free of charge, their current defense spending patterns and inventories indicate that they could not maintain and operate the equipment properly. The funds required to operate a squadron of aircraft such as F-16s and F-18s in a manner approaching NATO training standards would again exceed or form a majority of the O&M share of these countries' total defense budgets.

What defense planning strategies would then be most effective for the MAP states? In view of the current benign security environment and the multitude of urgent needs connected with integrating their military establishments into NATO, putting off any procurement of combat aircraft for now makes sense. A reasonable alternative, with long-term integration in mind, is to reduce inventory through a massive phase-out of existing assets, modernize one or two types of combat aircraft in the current inventory, and lease or purchase small numbers of used F-16s or F-18s (also implementing NATO training and doctrine and making much greater use of simulators).[9] These steps will begin the process of achieving greater compatibility with NATO operations.

In this light, Romania may have acted prudently by delaying its procurement of new combat aircraft for a decade and proceeding instead with a thorough modernization of the MiG-21 to secure its air sovereignty in the near- and medium-term. This decision will prove especially useful if it allows for more intensive and NATO-style training and thus provides for an interim period of familiarity with

---

[9]Since 1996, the United States has offered Poland, the Czech Republic, and Hungary a no-cost five-year lease of small numbers of either F-16s or F-18s, with the lessees paying for setting up the necessary infrastructure, training, and spares. For a variety of reasons, none of the three countries has yet taken up the offer, though the deal would allow for a gradual transition to a NATO-type aircraft. A five-year lease of 18 used aircraft to Poland has been estimated to cost approximately $200 million. (Andrew Doyle, "Pole Position," *Flight International*, April 28–May 4, 1999, pp. 42–44.) As of late 2000, an agreement on a transfer of 16 F-16A/Bs to Poland, together with an upgrade package, appeared to have been reached.

NATO tactics and doctrine.[10] However, the modernization of the MiG-21s must be accompanied by a large inventory reduction in the Romanian air force if there are to be O&M savings that can then be applied to increased training and readiness. Bulgaria's plans to withdraw from service all but its MiG-29s and Su-25s follow the pattern of the three NATO members that joined in 1999 and represent a move in the right direction. In contrast, Slovakia's continued use of small numbers of several combat aircraft types raises questions about the maintenance burden of such an inventory and suggests that a streamlining process is in order.

As for the "emerging" MAP militaries, their air forces are miniscule compared with those of Bulgaria, Romania, and Slovakia. Estonia, Latvia, Lithuania, Macedonia, and Slovenia have little equipment of any kind, much less jet combat aircraft. Given these countries' low defense budgets, their procurement of supersonic combat aircraft is neither realistic nor advisable. Tables A.4 through A.8, in the Appendix, provide details about these five MAP countries' air force inventories. An inventory of the Albanian air force is also included, as Table A.9, in the Appendix. Albania properly belongs within the oversize group but has divested itself of its air force by allowing it to fall into a state of disrepair and non-serviceability and thus fits the "emerging" pattern at this point.

Training

Slovakia, Romania, and Bulgaria face similar, if more severe, training problems than were encountered by Poland, the Czech Republic, and Hungary. Indeed, although the equipment modernization problems facing these three oversized MAP armed forces are undoubtedly serious, the low serviceability of aircraft and limited training available to their aircrews are much more serious. Current levels of flight hours for pilots in Slovakia, Romania, and Bulgaria

---

[10]The Romanian modernization program covers 110 MiG-21s (first batch delivered in 1997) and includes advanced avionics and PGM capabilities for ground support and Rafael Python 3 and R-73 air-to-air missiles (AAMs) for air defense. In addition, a new training program for aircrews is supposed to be modeled on training methods in NATO countries. ("Military Aviation Review: Romania," *World Airpower Journal*, 31, Winter 1997.)

range from 30 to 45 hours per year.[11] In contrast, the three members that joined in 1999 have raised their flying hours to 100 (or more) per year for a select group of aircrews assigned to NATO command and plan to increase these rates further, to 160 to 180 hours, by 2002. Since NATO expects 180 to 240 flight hours in its air forces, the figures in the MAP states seem barely adequate to ensure basic flight proficiency. The low training levels will have consequences down the road, making joint operations and integration of these air forces into NATO difficult.

The problems defy easy solutions because of the incompatibility in aircraft design and doctrine of the former communist states and NATO. To give one example, the Soviet-designed aircraft are expensive to operate and maintain compared with the main NATO-type aircraft. Some of the elements of the Soviet aircraft are rugged but require frequent maintenance; for example, the overhaul levels for their engines are three to four times those for the engines in NATO's main combat aircraft. Such aircraft would be extremely costly to operate if aircrew training were to approach the levels expected by NATO. Moreover, the aircraft were designed for short-range missions with a doctrinal emphasis on ground-control guidance rather than pilot initiative. This doctrine will have to change and aircrews will have to be used differently if these forces are to realize a payoff from increased training. Such training will be enormously expensive, however. One option is to attain higher training levels by re-engineering the MiG-29s to lower their high operating costs. Nevertheless, design limitations mean that aircraft such as MiG-29s, even if made compatible, are far from ideal platforms in a NATO environment. After a certain point, the costs of extensive modernization begin to look questionable compared with the costs of used F-16s or F-18s.

The implication of this discussion is that equipment, and especially the potential procurement of new combat aircraft by the former communist states, cannot be seen in isolation from improved training and adoption of NATO air doctrine. Substantial investments are needed in both areas. Even with optimal investments, it will be

---

[11]The country-specific data are as follows: Bulgaria, 30 to 40; Romania, 40; and Slovakia, 45 (*The Military Balance*, 2000–01. London: International Institute for Strategic Studies).

many years before the aspiring members reach the standards of versatility and proficiency common among the pre-1990 NATO members. The oversized MAP armed forces will have the more difficult time meeting NATO training standards, unless they use their resources optimally. None of the problems is unexpected or insurmountable, but all will take time and effort to overcome.

Equipment: Support Aircraft

Three of the oversized MAP air forces—those of Slovakia, Romania, and Bulgaria—have some small and mid-size transport aircraft (An-24s and An-26s in all three states, and several C-130s in Romania) that could play a role in NATO operations. However, these aircraft suffer from the same serviceability and training problems that apply to combat aircraft. Their usefulness appears limited to supply operations in support of any of their ground-force contingents that may be participating in NATO peace operations. None of the MAP states has tanker aircraft or early warning aircraft suitable for operations in a NATO framework.

Equipment: Army Aviation

The experience of Poland, the Czech Republic, and Hungary indicates that the problems affecting fixed-wing aircraft may apply to a lesser degree to rotary-wing aircraft. A Czech helicopter detachment took part in NATO's Implementation Force (IFOR) operations in Bosnia-Herzegovina, and Czech Mi-17s took part in March 2000 in a NATO field-training exercise in northern Norway in extremely demanding winter conditions. Polish utility helicopters have taken part in joint exercises with NATO units, and all three new members intend to assign helicopters (transport and combat) to NATO's planned Immediate Reaction Task Force Land (IRTF [L]). Since Slovakia and Bulgaria have equipment similar to that of these three newest NATO members, a similar contribution can be reasonably expected from them. The main combat helicopters of the three new members and Slovakia and Bulgaria are Mi-24s, rugged aircraft that still retain combat potential and could be a force multiplier in NATO's operations in the Balkans. Modernized Romanian IAR-330s, which are based on a French design, should be even easier to fit into NATO operations. None of this is to downplay the problems associated with compatibility, spare parts, and training that have affected army aviation in the three new members and the oversized MAP armed forces, but the experience does suggest that army aviation may be a more achievable pathway to a meaningful air contribution and a natural complement to a ground forces focus for the MAP states.

Equipment: SAMs

In terms of medium- and high-altitude surface-to-air missiles (SAMs), the three oversized MAP armed forces follow the pattern of Polish, Czech, and Hungarian forces, though Romania's holdings are not as modern. Tables 5.4 and 5.5 provide an inventory of SAM holdings that have more than tactical capabilities (excluding man-portable and self-propelled low-altitude SAMs) for the MAP states and the new members, respectively.

Other than Bulgaria, Slovakia, and Romania, the MAP states have neither combat aircraft nor SAMs capable of posing a threat to aircraft flying at altitudes over 10,000 feet. As such, they currently have no means of their own to ensure sovereignty over their airspace.[12]

Table 5.4

Medium- and High-Altitude SAM Inventory, 1999: MAP States

State	SA-2	SA-3	SA-4	SA-5	SA-6	SA-10
Albania	X[a]					
Bulgaria	X	X	X	X	X	X
Estonia						
Latvia						
Lithuania						
Macedonia						
Romania	X	X			X	
Slovakia	X	X		X	X	X
Slovenia						

SOURCE: IISS, *Jane's*.
[a]Serviceability questionable.

---

[12]Lithuania has some L-39 (subsonic) armed jet trainers, giving it a symbolic means of ensuring its own air sovereignty.

Table 5.5

Medium- and High-Altitude SAM Inventory, 1999:
New (1999) NATO Members

State	SA-2	SA-3	SA-4	SA-5	SA-6	SA-10
Czech Republic	X	X		X	X	
Hungary	X	X	X	X	X	
Poland	X	X^a	X	X^a	X^a	

SOURCE: IISS, *Jane's.*
^{a}Modernized.

Airspace and Infrastructure

The greatest contribution that the MAP countries can make to NATO's future air operations is to allow NATO uninhibited access to their airspace and to provide the infrastructure needed to support NATO's missions in and around Europe. Access to bases in these countries can extend the operational range of USAF combat aircraft operating in central, eastern, and southeastern Europe and decrease the need for aerial refueling. Figures 5.1 and 5.2 are maps illustrating the availability of airfields suitable for NATO use (permanent-surface runways that are in good condition and over 8,000 feet in length) in the northern and southern MAP and new member states. Runways over 8,000 feet are generally adequate for fighter operations and strategic airlift (of course, not all airfields with longer runways have adequate ramp space to support airlift operations). The maps are far from exhaustive, as there are many airfields in the 6,000 to 8,000 foot range that could be used for NATO operations. There are also other airfields, currently assessed to be in less than good condition, that could be brought rapidly to operational levels.

The accession of Poland, Hungary, and the Czech Republic has already provided much geostrategic depth to NATO, especially in the north. Access to Polish airspace and bases has given NATO the reach needed for hypothetical contingencies in the Baltic Sea littoral or the western part of the former USSR. Access to Czech infrastructure is useful from the perspective of supporting NATO operations in Poland, and access to bases in Hungary (Taszar and Budapest-Ferihegy) already has proved useful in NATO's peace operations in the former Yugoslavia. But the Kosovo air operation showed the value of access to Slovak, Romanian, and Bulgarian airspace. In fact, the closing of Romanian and Bulgarian airspace to Russian air transports at a crucial time probably saved NATO an acute confrontation with Russia in the final stages of Operation Allied Force. In the future, unconstrained access to Romanian and Bulgarian bases would be especially useful in case of contingencies in the Black Sea littoral, the former Yugoslavia, Moldova, or Ukraine. Should bases in or access to airspace over Turkey or Greece be unavailable, the value of Romania and Bulgaria for NATO operations would increase (as was the case during Operation Allied Force, when NATO's access to Greek airspace was limited). Access to Slovak airspace (in conditions of no access to Austrian airspace) is important, as it provides a link to Hungary from the northern NATO countries and allows greater depth for operations by support aircraft (tanker aircraft during Operation Allied Force).

The experience with new members sheds some light on the state of infrastructure in the MAP countries. NATO has ruled out explicitly the permanent basing of air or ground units in new member states under the conditions of the current benign security environment. If that environment continues to hold, the infrastructures of the new NATO countries will be used only for temporary and occasional training deployments by forces from other NATO countries. Of course, if the security environment were to change for the worse, the infrastructures of the new member states might become important for other NATO members' air forces, including the USAF. But the more likely scenario is that the infrastructures of new members will become important for NATO air forces by way of NATO's stability operations and conflict prevention. In this sense, the MAP states' infrastructures could be used for USAF forward operating or support locations.[13]

Currently, few bases in the MAP states meet all NATO standards for safe operations. However, most of the needed improvements are minor (for example, navigational aids) and could be made quickly if needed. Detailed NATO surveys of airbases in the MAP states, as well

---

[13]Paul S. Killingsworth, Lionel Galway, Eiichi Kamiya, Brian Nichiporuk, Timothy L. Ramey, Robert S. Tripp, and James C. Wendt, *Flexbasing: Achieving Global Presence for Expeditionary Aerospace Forces*, RAND, MR-1113-AF, 2000.

Figure 5.1—Map Showing Infrastructure: Northern New Member
and MAP States

Figure 5.2—Map Showing Infrastructure: Southern New Member
and MAP States

as experience with the similarly structured bases in the three new
member states, provide the necessary data on what to expect and
what is needed. Even without such improvements, NATO operations
from bases in MAP states are feasible with a little advance planning
and preparation. On a number of occasions, both pre- and post-
accession, U.S. and other NATO aircraft and command elements
have deployed to bases on the new members' territory and operated

jointly with their air forces in exercises.[14] As part of the NATO integration process and PfP cooperation, the individual MAP states have taken steps during the past few years to upgrade selected airfields to full NATO standards. Gradually, most of the operational airfields in these countries will meet all NATO flight safety requirements.

In a process that dates back to 1992, the United States has assisted all the new NATO member and MAP countries in setting up a NATO-compatible network of air sovereignty, early warning, and air traffic control centers (ASOCs). By late 2000, the ASOCs in all the MAP states either were operational or were to become operational shortly. Modernization of the system on a regional basis will ease these countries' integration into NATO's integrated air defense system if and when they become members, and will allow for safe operations in their airspace.[15]

Finally, many new and potential members have made training areas available for NATO aircraft. Given the restrictions in most of NATO Europe on aerial training (and especially on low-altitude training), access to new training grounds nearby amounts to a significant asset. Moreover, urban sprawl and the consequent public pressure to restrict aerial training areas have not progressed in most of the MAP countries to anywhere near the levels of western Europe. The regular deployment of USAF combat aircraft to the Kuchyna-Malacky base in Slovakia has provided USAF training benefits (while also serving a shaping function with regard to Slovakia).

---

[14]For example, already in 1997, the United States deployed F-16s and F-15s to Powidz, Poland, for several days of U.S.-Polish exercises. Elements of USAFE's deployable air operations center were set up in Poland in support of combined assets from USAFE, U.S. Air National Guard, and the Polish Air Force.

[15]The initiative began modestly in 1992, with a U.S. effort to assist then Czechoslovakia, Poland, and Hungary in creating joint civil-military air traffic control systems. In 1994, it expanded to a major U.S. assistance program, the Regional Airspace Initiative (RAI), and within a few years was enlarged to cover most of the former communist countries in central Europe. By 1998, the RAI had developed to the point of creating a modern regional system of airspace management compatible with NATO's integrated air defense system and included 13 countries: Poland, the Czech Republic, Hungary, Slovakia, Austria, Slovenia, Romania, Bulgaria, Albania, Macedonia, Lithuania, Latvia, and Estonia. Although the ASOCs included in the program contain U.S. surveillance equipment (FPS-117 radars), indigenous designs have been adapted to fit within the new system.

THE FORMER NEUTRALS

The group of former European neutrals[16] that potentially could seek admission to NATO in the next 10 to 15 years would face processes of adjustment different from those of the former communist states. NATO has less influence over the force plans of these countries, which already have a virtual NATO membership through their EU affiliation and do not perceive themselves as depending directly on NATO to safeguard their long-term security. The air assets of these countries—Austria, Sweden, and Finland—are relatively easy to integrate into NATO (Finland, with some ex-Soviet equipment, is a partial exception), and their training is comparable to that of current NATO members. In addition, they bring with them access to training grounds (in northern Sweden and Finland) that allow extended low-altitude operations, and NATO air forces already use regularly the northern Swedish training areas. The quality of their infrastructure is also comparable to that of current NATO members, and they are all affluent, able to afford the changes necessary to be effective NATO members.

For these countries, the top shaping priority is to enable their air forces to participate in at least some of NATO's air operations, which would entail preparing deployable air assets and making doctrinal and training changes as necessary to fit into NATO operations. For example, if a Swedish air component were to operate from a non-Swedish airbase as part of a NATO operation, it would have to be logistically compatible with the NATO forces, sustainable outside its home base, and operated by personnel familiar with and proficient in all NATO procedures pertaining to flight operations. Another priority would be to preserve the capabilities of these air forces if the countries did indeed become NATO members. Sweden and to a lesser extent Finland might be tempted to reduce the level of resources they devote to defense, and air forces specifically, if their security were guaranteed within the NATO framework. However, the means available to NATO for influencing these three countries to adjust their air forces for NATO operations are limited. Consequently, the three are not bound by any mechanisms to adjust to NATO's

---

[16]The term *neutral* has lost its meaning in the post–Cold War world; the more accurate term, and one preferred by the former neutrals, is *non-aligned*.

wishes and, if they choose to do so, may retain air forces suited only to national needs.

FINAL CONSIDERATIONS

If one accepts the rationale behind NATO's transformation and enlargement, the fact that the MAP states' potential military contribution to NATO will remain low for the foreseeable future represents neither a major problem nor a shortcoming in relation to the political goal of re-unifying Europe and erasing the damage done by communism—and doing so on terms established by NATO and the EU. Nor is a low contribution all that unusual within NATO. Two long-standing NATO members contribute little (Luxembourg) or nothing (Iceland) in terms of military forces. Other members, such as Portugal, are not major political and military actors within NATO. The contribution of the MAP states is designated as low only when seen in an absolute sense. In relative terms, such as the defense effort and the ratio of troops assigned to NATO as a percentage of population, the MAP states have incentives to contribute forces at or above the median NATO level, because of their perceived insecurity and their need to make themselves valuable to NATO.

The important goal, and one where the shaping strategy comes into play, is to ensure that the MAP states use their scarce defense resources wisely and contribute in an optimal fashion to NATO. Recommendations for strategies are discussed at greater length in Chapter Six.

The problems associated with integrating the militaries of new members are neither insurmountable nor unexpected. NATO has added members several times previously, and each time the process typically has taken many years. Integration difficulties stem from NATO's having existed for five decades and its consequent institutionalization (and the ever-increasing number of NATO Standardization Agreements, or STANAGs), the increasing technological complexity of NATO's equipment and weapons, and the relative divergence of new members from NATO's norms. It took years for the West German armed forces to become integrated into NATO after Germany joined NATO. And the integration of the East German armed forces into unified German forces and a part of NATO seemed such a difficult task that it was not even attempted, and the East

German military (NVA) was in effect disbanded.[17] Ten years after German unification, only a fraction of the former professional NVA soldiers remained in the German armed forces,[18] and most for-mer NVA equipment had been scrapped or exported.

Unified Germany had the luxury of not needing to integrate the East German forces (indeed, for reasons of ensuring unification on West German terms, Germany had every reason to retain as few former NVA soldiers as possible), but the other former communist states in Europe that have joined or are on track to joining NATO have not had the same luxury. These countries have had to transform their militaries into institutions supportive of and capable of functioning in the new democratic environment while radically reducing their armed forces' resources and manpower. And they have had to do so while simultaneously attempting to retain their basic defense capabilities and become an integrated part of a military alliance with its own mode of operation.[19] Those former communist countries that attained sovereignty in the early 1990s also faced other problems, since they had to set up their armed forces either from scratch or from predecessor-state forces. In both cases, the sheer magnitude of the change has no easy parallels.[20]

---

[17]For more on the disbanding of the NVA and integration of its remnants into the Bundeswehr, see Joerg Schoenbohm, *Two Armies and One Fatherland: The End of the Nationale Volksarmee*, Providence and Oxford: Berghahn Books, 1996; Dale R. Herspring, *Requiem for an Army: The Demise of the East German Military*, Lanham, Maryland: Rowman and Littlefield, 1998.

[18]In 1998, there were 4,797 former NVA soldiers serving in the Bundeswehr, of which 1,343 were officers and the rest NCOs. The NVA comprised 100,000 to 120,000 soldiers in 1989–90. (Data for 1998 are from Dale R. Herspring, "From the NVA to the Bundeswehr: Bringing the East Germans into NATO," in Andrew A. Michta, *America's New Allies: Poland, Hungary, and the Czech Republic in NATO*, Seattle and London: University of Washington Press, 1999, p. 34.)

[19]For an analytical review of the experience of integrating the three countries that joined NATO in 1999, see Andrew A. Michta, "Poland: A Linchpin of Regional Security," pp. 40–73; Zoltan Barany, "Hungary: An Outpost on the Troubled Periphery," pp. 74–111; Thomas S. Szayna, "The Czech Republic: A Small Contributor or a 'Free Rider'?" pp. 112–148, in Andrew A. Michta, *America's New Allies: Poland, Hungary, and the Czech Republic in NATO*, Seattle and London: University of Washington Press, 1999; Congressional Budget Office, "Integrating New Allies into NATO," Paper, Washington, D.C., October 2000.

[20]German unification is not a good parallel, since it amounted to the disbanding of the NVA. The evolution of the Finnish defense establishment in the 1990s offers some insights on what a country that was formerly a heavy user of Soviet equipment can

After a decade of military reform, the integration problems faced by the three new members and the MAP countries have been scrutinized in great detail. Whether it comes to training, equipment, or, perhaps more important than all, the human dimension, there is already voluminous literature on the existing problems and the remedies needed.[21] But the overwhelming nature of the task and the novelty of some of the problems mean that putting together an effective strategy for transformation of the MAP militaries is not easy. This is where NATO's shaping incentives come into play and can have a major influence, as discussed in the next chapter.

---

accomplish. With proper planning and affluent conditions (and the resulting relative availability of resources), the Finnish defense establishment implemented a shift away from its position as a Cold War–era "neutral" highly sensitive to Soviet concerns to a country integrated into the EU and the larger EU/NATO defense community. The extent of the shift within the Finnish defense establishment is especially striking in view of the data coming out of the post–Cold War opening of the archives, which show that Finland's status during the Cold War was akin to that of a semi-satellite of the USSR. For example, on Soviet influence over the Finnish media, see Esko Salminen, *The Silenced Media: The Propaganda War Between Russia and the West in Northern Europe*, New York: St. Martin's Press, 1999.

[21]David Glantz's study of the training and educational problems facing the Polish, Czech, and Hungarian militaries and suggestions for addressing them is probably the most comprehensive so far. Its recommendations have much relevance for the MAP countries. The Glantz study was reprinted in three parts in *The Journal of Slavic Military Studies*: "Military Training and Education Challenges in Poland, the Czech Republic, and Hungary," 11:3, September 1998, pp. 1–55 (part 1); "The Accomplishments, Strengths and Weaknesses of the U.S. Military (Security) Assistance Program," 11:4, December 1998, pp. 1–71 (part 2); "Military Training and Educational Challenges in Poland, the Czech Republic and Hungary; Conclusions and Recommendations," 12:1, March 1999, pp. 1–12 (part 3). Other good studies or analyses include Christina M. Patterson, David R. Markov, and Karen J. Richter, *Western-Style Armaments for New NATO Countries*, Institute for Defense Analyses, P–3450, June 1999; Brigadier-General Michael H. Clemmesen, "Integration of New Alliance Members: The Intellectual-Cultural Dimension," *Defense Analysis*, 15:3, 1999, pp. 261–272. For suggestions concerning a policy on the sale of arms to the former communist countries, see Dov S. Zakheim, "Rationalizing and Coordinating the Sale of Conventional Armaments in Central and Eastern Europe," *International Politics*, 34, September 1997, pp. 303–326. New member and MAP militaries also have examined nearly every imaginable aspect of military integration into NATO. The professional military press, especially the Polish *Mysl Wojskowa* and the Czech *Vojenske Rozhledy*, has published many assessments along these lines.

Chapter Six

CONCLUSIONS

NATO's post–Cold War enlargement has provoked a heated debate on the wisdom of enlargement and NATO's eventual composition. The 1999 accession of three new members and NATO's identification of nine states as on track to membership have led some analysts to caution that NATO's cohesion is at risk.[1] Although these concerns are real, the fears are probably exaggerated. NATO's founding document defines the alliance as open to all European states sharing its values, and until NATO's members modify that clause, it remains in force. But being open to new membership does not in any way obligate NATO to accept new members, especially if current members judge an accession to be damaging to the overall security environment.

As a result, the existence of countries that aspire to NATO membership does not mean that all or even more than a few of them will be admitted to NATO in the foreseeable future. NATO's elaborate criteria for new members have established a high standard for aspiring states, one that several (at least four) of its pre-1990 members cannot meet. Moreover, NATO explicitly stated in its 1995 enlargement study that it is up to NATO members to decide if and when additional states will be invited. The analysis in this report suggests that

---

[1]Some analysts are supportive of enlargement but worry about the pace of the process and its impact on NATO's ability to undertake military operations (Hans Binnendijk and Richard L. Kugler, "Open NATO's Door Carefully," *The Washington Quarterly*, 22:2, Spring 1999, pp. 125–138). Others fear that the process will fall prey to its own dynamics and detach completely from any strategic rationale (Karl-Heinz Kamp, "NATO Entrapped: Debating the Next Enlargement Round," *Survival*, 40:3, Autumn 1998, pp. 170–186).

if the current security trends continue, NATO's membership will grow, because NATO is now institutionally committed to the concept of enlargement, and the enlargement process is one of the pillars of and strengthens the benign security environment that now exists in Europe. However, the pace of enlargement will be gradual and will pose no threat to NATO's cohesion or its ability to engage in military operations in Europe.

Probably the most significant element of NATO's post–Cold War adaptation is not its enlargement but its transformation, which entails acceptance of a power projection role and the unilateral assumption of responsibility for European security, broadly defined. This transformation has wide implications for European security. Tellingly, it was NATO's embracing of new missions, such as Operation Allied Force, that caused a rupture in its relations with Russia—something that several years of debate over enlargement and NATO's admittance of three countries in 1999 had not managed to do.

NATO's enlargement and its transformation both aim to shape the political environment in Europe. Each has already profoundly and beneficially affected the security environment in Europe's unintegrated area by establishing incentives for cooperative approaches to security and encouraging democratic reforms. Through the mechanics of enlargement, NATO has established not only a multitude of channels for cooperation with non-members, but also gray-area commitments that, in and of themselves, given the reigning preponderance of NATO military power in Europe, safeguard the sovereignty of some of the smaller and more insecure states in Europe's unintegrated area without provoking a Russian response and allow their further democratic development.

The enlargement process has, however, created complications for defense planning. During the 1997–99 round of enlargement, NATO extended a membership invitation to Hungary, Poland, and the Czech Republic, the three countries seemingly least in need of its security guarantee. The seeming paradox shows the prominence of the political shaping motivations behind enlargement, NATO's overall cautious attitude, and the preferences of NATO's key members. The paradox has remained and indeed has become stronger because of how enlargement has unfolded. Through MAP, NATO has singled out several countries as possible future NATO members, in effect giving them an implicit security guarantee for the interim period. From a defense planning perspective, the current paradox lies in the fact that the MAP countries least in need of such an implicit guarantee are the most likely to be admitted to NATO in the near- and mid-term, while those most in need of NATO's security guarantee (because they cannot provide much of a deterrent in case of unexpected contingencies) are the least likely to be admitted in the near- or mid-term.

The hypothetical contingencies envisioned are not all catastrophic shocks to the system; they could involve less drastic changes along the lines suggested by the branch points of uncertainty-sensitive planning. Since NATO's condition of a gray-area commitment is likely to last for a considerable length of time, there is more likelihood that some of the branch-point shifts may come to pass. The complication is that for this decade and perhaps beyond, NATO has provided a "soft" guarantee to countries with little indigenous ability to provide for their own deterrent.

While this problem is generally recognized, the fact that the rationale behind enlargement is primarily political means that the challenges it creates for military planning may be underemphasized. For example, when Poland, the Czech Republic, and Hungary acceded in 1999, no less than the former chairman of the NATO Military Committee, General Klaus Naumann, informally expressed concerns about extending security guarantees to these countries because of interoperability problems and NATO's potential lack of military capability for meeting such a commitment.[2] The extension of soft security guarantees to the MAP states has intensified the problem, as many of the MAP countries have limited means to defend their territory against any modern adversary. In such conditions, these countries are susceptible to military blackmail, to operations by aggressor units not under governmental authority, or to any number of other contingencies short of a full-scale invasion.

Recognition of these problems should not be construed as an argument against enlargement. The very extension of a soft security

---

[2]As reported in Simon Brossard, "Altered Alliance," *Flight International*, April 28–May 4, 1999, p. 32.

guarantee may have succeeded—for now—in ensuring the sovereignty of the MAP countries without provoking a Russian response strong enough to affect the overall security environment. However, as stated above, the move does present complications for planning.

From the U.S. Air Force's perspective, the complication perhaps most relevant is that except for Slovakia, Romania, and Bulgaria (with their oversized militaries), none of the MAP states has the means even to ensure its own air sovereignty. Nor do they have any near- or even mid-term prospects for acquiring these means—short of NATO countries assuming the role for them. One of the few plausible ways for these states to gain their own air sovereignty capabilities is for them to lease or cascade NATO aircraft, once they are capable of fully operating such aircraft and affording the support packages. However, a better alternative (especially in the case of the emerging militaries) is for them to allocate their resources efficiently by prioritizing near-term investment choices toward well-trained and equipped ground forces (with their own air defense—SAM—capabilities). Such forces would provide a non-provocative credible deterrent and enable these states to make a real contribution to NATO's peace operations. Moreover, in the unexpected event that the current benign security environment changes for the worse and a MAP state falls into crisis, a fully NATO-interoperable core of ground forces (including ground air controllers) could provide initial defense of the country's borders, with NATO quickly deploying its air assets to reinforce the MAP state in crisis, and NATO ground forces arriving later.

In an overall sense, none of the MAP states can be expected to contribute in any meaningful fashion to NATO's air operations for the near- and mid-term. If the oversized militaries proceed with far-reaching military reform, they may—with proper guidance from NATO—be able to contribute some air assets (especially army aviation) to NATO operations in the mid-term. Potentially of greatest use to NATO is access to MAP state airspace and infrastructure, which could be used for NATO operations in the Balkans, potential contingencies, and training.

Under a continuation of the no-surprises security environment in Europe, the challenges inherent to NATO's enlargement will not amount to a major problem. It is entirely plausible that over the next 10 to 15 years, the main missions of the U.S. armed forces in Europe will consist primarily of shaping the environment and assisting in the integration of new and potential members and partners, interrupted occasionally by humanitarian missions, peacekeeping, and perhaps even coercive peacemaking (as in Operation Allied Force). However, a benign no-surprises future is in no way guaranteed and cannot be taken for granted in elaborating a shaping strategy. Even without a major shock to the European security environment, NATO's transformation and enlargement both contain internal logic problems that may change the calculations of a future European security environment in non-trivial ways. NATO's transformation has led to a heightened collective action problem that reduces NATO's cohesion, and NATO's enlargement strategy has assumed that new members will institutionalize its pre-admission criteria and share its need to engage Russia—neither of which may hold true over the long-term. As the formulators of uncertainty-sensitive planning have stated, "Perhaps China will never invade Taiwan and perhaps Russia will never invade Lithuania, but if we consider the long list of strategically plausible events and realize that some of them *will* occur, then our approach to strategy will be different."[3]

SHAPING DETERMINANTS

An appropriate shaping policy for the United States and its allies must include a hedging strategy. With this in mind, an effective shaping strategy for MAP states should be individually tailored and should incorporate an understanding of five key issues:[4]

1. The extent of the potential strategic exposure and need for NATO reinforcement that accompany hypothetical threats to a MAP state under crisis conditions.

2. The time frame for a MAP state likely joining NATO.

---

[3]Paul K. Davis and Zalmay M. Khalilzad, *A Composite Approach to Air Force Planning*, RAND, MR-787-AF, 1996, p. 18.

[4]For an overview of the larger shaping priorities for NATO as a whole, see David A. Ochmanek, *NATO's Future: Implications for U.S. Military Capabilities and Posture*, RAND, MR-1162-AF, 2000.

3. The severity of the problems a MAP state faces with its armed forces (including the difference between "oversized" and "emerging" militaries, which also indicates how applicable the lessons learned from NATO's integration of Poland, the Czech Republic, and Hungary will be).

4. The means available to a MAP state for addressing the problems of its armed forces.

5. The likely useful (technologically sophisticated and well-trained) contribution of a MAP state to NATO's peace operations.

These issues represent the main determinants for a NATO shaping strategy. The information can be presented by way of a "radar chart," as shown in Figure 6.1, with each country graded on a high-medium-low scale for each issue. Country A presents a case of difficult combinations. It has a high level of strategic exposure and low likelihood of NATO membership in the near-term, severe problems with its armed forces and a low level of resources available to deal with such problems, and a low potential contribution to NATO's peace operations in the near- and mid-term. In all, country A combines a high level of vulnerability in conditions of a lengthy implied NATO security guarantee with severe military problems and low availability to address those problems on its own. In contrast, country B presents more favorable combinations. It has a low level of strategic exposure and a high likelihood of NATO membership in the near-term, medium-level problems with its armed forces and a medium level of resources available to deal with those problems, and a non-trivial likely contribution to NATO's peace operations.

The two countries require different types of NATO shaping policies. NATO has to plan with some urgency on assisting country A in building up a minimum deterrence capability so as to decrease the level of strategic exposure in conditions of a continued MAP-like "gray area" security guarantee. In view of the severity of the military problems experienced by country A and its low level of resources, NATO may need to provide equipment and training at low or no cost. Since country A is not going to be a major contributor to NATO's peace operations, the focus of NATO's efforts should be on deterrence and home defense, with any contribution to peace operations accruing as a side benefit of building up the MAP military.

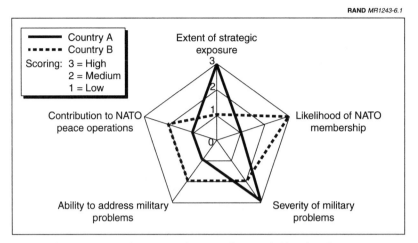

Figure 6.1—Main Determinants of a NATO Shaping Strategy

In contrast, the low strategic exposure of country B and its likely near-term membership in NATO mean that NATO's efforts with regard to this country lack the sense of urgency present in its efforts with regard to country A. Moreover, NATO can expect country B to take the primary role in addressing its relatively limited military problems. The focus of the military reform efforts should be on making a contribution to NATO's peace operations rather than on deterrence and home defense. From the perspective of NATO military planning, country B presents fewer complications. But even though country A presents more complications for NATO military planning, it is more important that its problems be dealt with in a timely fashion, since addressing them reduces the country's strategic exposure and thus the likelihood of its being involved in a crisis that could necessitate NATO's intervention.

Figures 6.2 through 6.10 individually portray the position of each MAP country in such a format. The data on which the ratings for each country are based are derived from assessments earlier in the report. Table 6.1 presents the numerical assessments.

As the charts in Figures 6.2 through 6.10 make clear, each of the MAP countries—even those usually lumped together, such as Estonia, Latvia, and Lithuania—differs from the others to some extent. It is

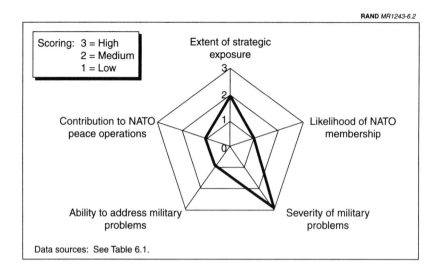

Figure 6.2—Main Determinants of a NATO Shaping Strategy: Albania

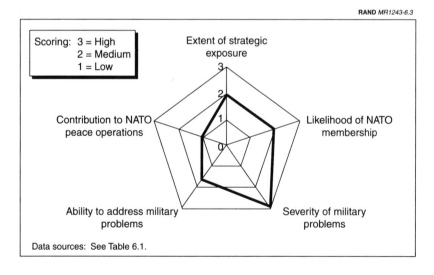

Figure 6.3—Main Determinants of a NATO Shaping Strategy: Bulgaria

RAND *MR1243-6.4*

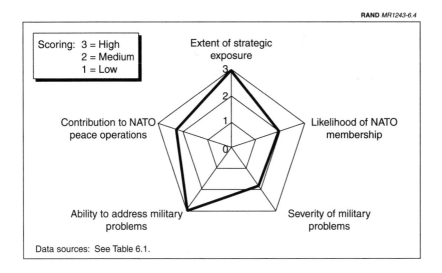

Figure 6.4—Main Determinants of a NATO Shaping Strategy: Estonia

RAND *MR1243-6.5*

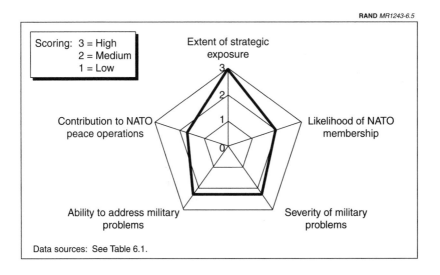

Figure 6.5—Main Determinants of a NATO Shaping Strategy: Latvia

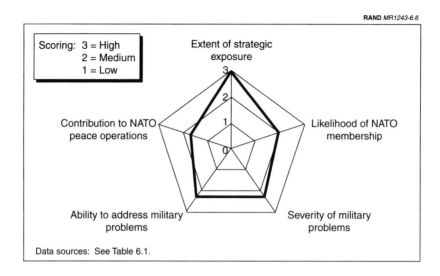

Figure 6.6—Main Determinants of a NATO Shaping Strategy: Lithuania

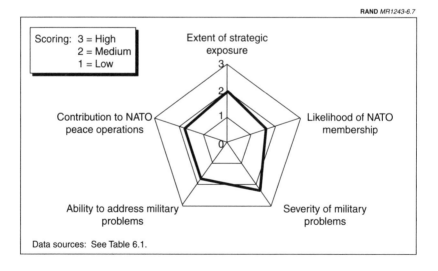

Figure 6.7—Main Determinants of a NATO Shaping Strategy: Macedonia

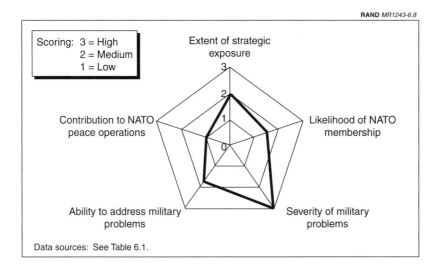

Figure 6.8—Main Determinants of a NATO Shaping Strategy: Romania

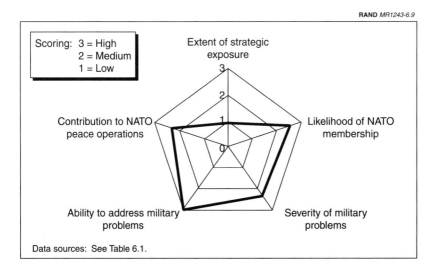

Figure 6.9—Main Determinants of a NATO Shaping Strategy: Slovakia

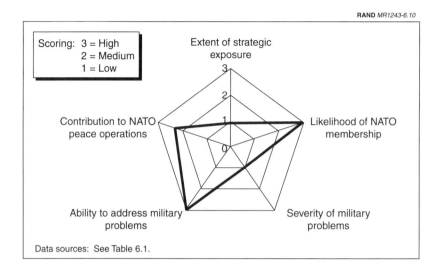

RAND MR1243-6.10

Figure 6.10—Main Determinants of a NATO Shaping Strategy: Slovenia

Table 6.1

Main Determinants of a NATO Shaping Strategy for the MAP States

State	Extent of Strategic Exposure[a]	Likelihood of NATO Member-ship[b]	Severity of Military Problems[c]	Ability to Address Military Problems[d]	Contribution to NATO Peace Ops[e]
Albania	2	1	3	1	1
Bulgaria	2	2	3	1.7	1
Estonia	3	2	1.7	3	2.3
Latvia	3	2	2.3	2.3	1.7
Lithuania	3	2	2.3	2.3	1.7
Macedonia	2	1.5	2.3	1.7	1.7
Romania	2	1.5	3	1.7	1
Slovakia	1	2.5	2.3	3	2.3
Slovenia	1	3	1	3	2.3

NOTE: Scoring is 1 = low; 2 = medium; 3 = high.
[a]Values derived from overall scores in Table 4.20, inverted.
[b]Values derived from overall scores in Table 4.26.
[c]Values derived from military scores in Table 4.16, adjusted to a 1–3 scale and inverted.
[d]Values derived from overall scores in Table 4.5.
[e]Values derived from power projection scores in Table 4.22.

important that NATO take these differences into account as it proceeds with a shaping strategy. They are essential to putting together the most effective strategy and thus advancing the no-surprises future in a most efficient fashion.

The oversized militaries of Slovakia, Romania, and Bulgaria bring with them the problem of their equipment, doctrine, and training levels all being incompatible with those of NATO. Nonetheless, all three of these MAP states have a deterrent force in place and have the means to ensure sovereignty over their airspace. The other six MAP states—Slovenia, Albania, Macedonia, Lithuania, Latvia, and Estonia—possess armed forces that may be insufficient for deterrence purposes (either because of quality, quantity, or both), and they have only embryonic air forces, meaning that in the event of an unexpected crisis, NATO may need to ensure their air sovereignty. The following recommendations and shaping guidelines take into account the different kinds of problems presented by the MAP militaries:

- To enhance NATO's air operations over the long-term, the highest priority for MAP states should be fundamental military reform that adapts the military to principles prevalent in current NATO countries. Without such a framework in place, cooperation with and assistance from NATO in force planning and development fail to meet a basic prerequisite for success.

- Defense investments need to be specifically directed at building a small core of well-equipped and trained light-weight and (for the "oversized" militaries) medium-weight ground forces that are fully compatible with NATO. If some recognized uncertainties were to come to pass, such forces would establish the foundation for a quick path to accession and/or NATO cooperation in conditions of crisis-time reinforcement, without committing NATO to such a path in advance.

- Specific priorities for the air forces should be as follows: The oversized MAP militaries should focus on rapidly reducing their inventories, modernizing (and adapting to NATO) their remaining assets, and reassigning their resources to training and readiness improvements. The emerging MAP militaries should focus on preparing the conditions for an eventual air component consisting of army aviation and/or combat-capable jet trainers. In

Lithuania, Latvia, and Estonia, regional arrangements (along the lines of a "Baltic" air force) would amount to a cost-effective way to ensure air sovereignty. The ability to monitor and control the use of one's airspace is a virtual prerequisite of sovereignty, and the MAP states will need to maintain a minimum level of credible counter-air capability.

- In both the oversized and emerging militaries, investments in niche areas, such as ground support aircraft (whether rotary- or fixed-wing) and tactical airlift, would be a natural complement to the focus on ground forces. In this context, army aviation and support assets—rather than the combat Soviet-type fixed-wing assets possessed by the new members and MAP states—could be deployed out of their home countries for NATO operations. Eventually, and especially for the oversized MAP militaries, a longer-term objective would be to field NATO-interoperable SAMs capable of posing a threat to aircraft at medium altitude so as to strengthen the air defense deterrent. Of course, a basic pre-requisite in all plans is compatibility with NATO doctrine, training, and equipment.

- In all MAP countries, the emphasis must be on infrastructure preparation (including the upgrading of select airbases usable for crisis-time reinforcement or for NATO peace operations) and the completion of an air traffic control and air sovereignty system that allow for full integration of the MAP states into NATO's air defense network. These two elements would be especially important under conditions of crisis-time reinforcement. For hedging purposes, planning needs to consider the exposure to hypothetical threats that the various MAP countries would face if the security environment were to deteriorate. In and of itself, such preparation increases the deterrent to intimidation and, in a non-provocative fashion, strengthens the chances that NATO will not need to act on its gray-area commitments.

As the 1999 accession of Poland, the Czech Republic, and Hungary shows, integration of the MAP militaries into NATO will be a long and difficult process, especially in the realm of air forces and air defense. But whatever priorities emerge and whatever their specific order, what is clearly needed is a long-term phased strategy of development and integration for new and potential members. None of the former communist countries is likely to be a major contributor to NATO's air operations in the near- or mid-term, but all can play a meaningful role (even in air operations) depending on the contingency. Especially in cases of "coalitions of the willing," their specific strengths in niche areas may make them disproportionately valuable to the operation. NATO has the leverage and the means of influence to help coordinate the MAP states' choices and to assist countries in working toward optimal use of their resources and capabilities.

INVENTORY OF AIRCRAFT AND HELICOPTERS IN THE MAP STATES

Table A.1

Inventory of Aircraft and Helicopters, 2000: Bulgaria

Role	Type	Current Total	First Delivery	Current Status[a]
Interceptor	MiG-23MF Flogger-B (+MiG-23UB Flogger-C)	5 (+5)		Being withdrawn
	MiG-23ML Flogger-G	10 or less		Being withdrawn
	MiG-23MLD Flogger-K	10 or less		Being withdrawn
	MiG-29 Fulcrum-A (+MiG-29UB Fulcrum-B)	17 (+4)	1988	
Air defense/attack	MiG-21MF Fishbed	10		Most non-operational
	MiG-21bis Fishbed-N (+MiG-21UM Mongol-B)	40 (+15)		Most non-operational (approx. 20 in service)
Attack	MiG-23BN Flogger-H	5	1976	Being withdrawn
	Su-22M4 Fitter-K (+Su-22UM3 Fitter-G)	18 (+3)	1984	Being withdrawn
	Su-25 Frogfoot-A (+Su-25UB Frogfoot-B)	35 (+4)	1986	
Reconnaissance	MiG-21R Fishbed-H	9		Many non-operational
	MiG-21MFR Fishbed	4		Many non-operational
Armed trainer	L-39ZA Albatros	26	1986	
Transport	An-24 Coke	2		
	An-26 Curl	5		
Combat helicopter	Mi-24 Hind-D	35	1982	Many non-operational
	Mi-24 Hind-E	5		Many non-operational
Assault helicopter	Mi-8 Hip	7		
	Mi-17 Hip	21		
Combat support helicopter	Mi-17PP Hip-K	4		
Navy helicopters	Mi-14PL/BT Haze-A -B	10	1981	
Other fixed-wing trainers	L-29 Delfin	50		Some non-flyable
Other fixed-wing: communications, utility, survey	(2) Tu-134A, (1) Yak-40, (8) LET-410UVP, (1) An-30	12		Yak-40 to be withdrawn; LET-410 delivered in 1990
Other helicopters: utility	(14) Mi-2 Hoplite, (6) Bell 206B	20		Mi-2 being withdrawn; Bell delivered in 1999–2000

SOURCE: *Jane's*, IISS, Teal Group Corporation.

NOTE: Inventory includes Bulgarian Military Air Forces and Bulgarian Naval Aviation.

[a]In 1999–2000, 60 percent of aircraft were reported to be non-operational (*Jane's*).

Table A.2

Inventory of Aircraft and Helicopters, 2000: Romania

Role	Type	Current Total	First Delivery	Current Status
Interceptor	MiG-23MF Flogger-B (+MiG-23UB Flogger-C)	30 (+5)	1978	
Air defense/attack	MiG-21M/MF Fishbed-J (+MiG-21UM/US Mongol-B)	150 (+30)		100 (+10) being upgraded to "Lancer" standard
	MiG-29 Fulcrum-A (+MiG-29UB Fulcrum-B)	15 (+3)	1989	
Attack	IAR-93 A/B Orao	73	1980/86	
Reconnaissance	MiG-21R Fishbed-H	10		Many non-operational
	Il-28 Beagle	12		Many non-operational
Armed trainer	L-39ZA Albatros	30	1981	
	IAR-99 Soim	14	1988	24 total on order
Transport	An-24 Coke	6		
	An-26 Curl	11		Many non-operational
	Il-18	2		
	C-130B Hercules	4	1996	
Assault helicopter	IAR-330 Puma	79		24 being upgraded
	IAR-316/316A Alouette III	99		
Navy helicopters	Mi-14PL Haze-A, IAR-316	7		
Other fixed-wing trainers	(30) L-29 Delfin, (10) IAR-28MA, (36) IAR-823	76		
Other fixed-wing: utility, survey	(2) B-707, (10) An-2, (3) An-30, (1) Tu-154	16		
Other helicopters: communications, utility	(12) IAR-317, (6) Mi-8/17 Hip, 6 Mi-2	24		

SOURCES: *Jane's*, IISS, Teal Group Corporation.

NOTE: Inventory includes Romanian Military Aviation and Romanian Naval Air Arm but not Romanian Police.

Table A.3

Inventory of Aircraft and Helicopters, 2000: Slovakia

Role	Type	Current Total	First Delivery	Current Status
Interceptor	MiG-29 Fulcrum-A (+MiG-29UB Fulcrum-B)	22 (+2)	1989	
Air defense/ attack	MiG-21MF Fishbed-J (+MiG-21UM/US Mongol-B)	30 (+8)		Most withdrawn or in storage (approx. 12+4 in service)
Attack	Su-22M4 Fitter-K (+Su-22UM3 Fitter-G)	17 (+3)	1984	
	Su-25K Frogfoot-A (+Su-25UBK Frogfoot-B)	11 (+1)	1984	
Combat support	L-39V Albatros	2	1976	
Armed trainer	L-39C/MS/ZA Albatros	16	1971/1991/1976 5 2 9	
Transport	An-24V Coke	2		
	An-26 Curl	2		
	LET-410MA/VP Turbolet	4 (2/2)		
Combat helicopter	Mi-24D Hind-D (+Mi-24DU Hind)	8 (+1)		
	Mi-24V Hind-E	10		
Combat support helicopters	(2) Mi-17Z-II Hip, (1) Mi-8PPA Hip-K	3		
Other fixed-wing trainers	(14) L-29 Delfin, (3) LET-410T	17		
Other fixed-wing: communications, survey	(1) Tu-154M/B2, (2) LET-410FG,	3		
Other helicopters: utility	(14) Mi-8T/P Hip-C, (15) Mi-17 Hip-H, (6) Mi-2 Hoplite	35		7 Mi-8T in storage

SOURCE: *Jane's*, IISS, Teal Group Corporation.

NOTE: Inventory includes Air Force and Air Defense Forces but not Slovak Police.

Table A.4

Inventory of Aircraft and Helicopters, 2000: Estonia

Role	Type	Current Total	First Delivery	Current Status
Utility fixed-wing	(2) An-2 Colt, (2) L-410UVP-1 Turbolet	4		
Utility helicopters	Mi-2 Hoplite, (4) Mi-8	7	Mi-2 in 1995	

SOURCE: *Jane's*, IISS, Teal Group Corporation.

NOTE: Inventory includes Estonian Army Aviation and Estonian Border Guard (in wartime subordinated to Air Force staff).

Table A.5

Inventory of Aircraft and Helicopters, 2000: Latvia

Role	Type	Current Total	First Delivery	Current Status
Utility fixed-wing	(1) LET L-410UVP Turbolet, (4) An-2 Colt	6	L-410 in 1992–93	
Utility helicopters	Mi-2 Hoplite	8	1995	Some non-operational

SOURCE: *Jane's*, IISS, Teal Group Corporation.

NOTE: Inventory includes Latvian Air Force but not Latvian Republican Guard.

Table A.6

Inventory of Aircraft and Helicopters, 2000: Lithuania

Role	Type	Current Total	First Delivery	Current Status
Armed trainers	L-39ZA/C Albatros	6 (2/4)	1993, 1998	
Transport	An-26RV Curl	3	1994	
	LET-410UVP Turbolet	2	1993	
Utility fixed-wing	An-2 Colt	6	1993	
Utility helicopters	(8) Mi-8T/MTV Hip-C -H, (4) Mi-2	12	Mi-8 in 1993, Mi-2 in 1996	

SOURCE: *Jane's*, IISS, Teal Group Corporation.

NOTE: Inventory includes Lithuanian Military Air Forces but not National Border and Home Guard.

Table A.7

Inventory of Aircraft and Helicopters, 2000: Macedonia

Role	Type	Current Total	First Delivery	Current Status
Assault helicopters	Mi-17 (Mi-8MTV) Hip-H	3	1994	
Utility fixed-wing	(3) Zlin 242L, (1) Raytheon Super King Air	4	242L in 1997	

SOURCE: *Jane's*, IISS, Teal Group Corporation.

NOTE: Inventory includes Macedonian Republic Army Aviation but not National Border and Home Guard.

Table A.8

Inventory of Aircraft and Helicopters, 2000: Slovenia

Role	Type	Current Total	First Delivery	Current Status
Armed trainer	Pilatus PC-9	12	1995	Being modernized
Transport	LET-410UVP-E Turbolet	1	1994	
	Pilatus PC-6/	2	1998	
Utility helicopters	(2) Bell 412HP, (1) Bell 412SP, (5) Bell 412EP, (3) B-206	11	B-412 in 1992–96	

SOURCE: *Jane's*, IISS, Teal Group Corporation.

NOTE: Inventory includes Slovene Military Aviation.

Table A.9

Inventory of Aircraft and Helicopters, 2000: Albania

Role	Type	Current Total	First Delivery	Current Status[a]
Interceptor	Chengdu F-7A [MiG-21]	22	1979	Many non-operational
Air defense/attack	Shenyang F-6 [MiG-19]	32	1965	Many non-operational
Attack	Shenyang F-5 (+FT-5) [MiG-17]	11+8	1961–62	No more than 14 (total) operational
Reconnaissance	Shenyang F-6 [MiG-19]	4	1965	Many non-operational
Transport	Y-5 [An-2]	17	1963	No more than 10 operational
	Il-14M	3		Operational status uncertain
Fixed-wing trainers	(13) F-2, (11) FT-2, (6) Nanchang CJ-6	30	1955–62	Many non-operational
Utility helicopters	(40) Z-5 [Mi-4], (4) Aerospatialle SA-319B Alouette III (1) Bell-222UT, (3) Eurocopter SA-350B	48		Many Z-5 non-operational (delivered in 1957); Alouettes delivered in 1995

SOURCE: *Jane's*, IISS, Teal Group Corporation.

NOTE: Inventory includes Albanian People's Army Air Force.

[a]Serviceability of all Albanian aircraft is in question as a result of civil unrest in 1997.

REFERENCES

Annual list of speeches by NATO officials, 1995; http://www.nato.int/docu/speech/sp95.htm (through sp98.htm).

Barany, Zoltan, "Hungary: An Outpost on the Troubled Periphery," in Andrew A. Michta, *America's New Allies: Poland, Hungary, and the Czech Republic in NATO*, Seattle and London: University of Washington Press, 1999, pp. 74–111.

Bennett, D. Scott, "Testing Alternative Models of Alliance Duration, 1816–1984," *American Journal of Political Science*, 41:3, July 1997, pp. 846–878.

Binnendijk, Hans, and Richard L. Kugler, "Open NATO's Door Carefully," *The Washington Quarterly*, 22:2, Spring 1999, pp. 125–138.

Boland, Frank (Head, Force Planning Section of NATO's Defense Planning and Operations Division), *NATO Review*, 46:3, Autumn 1998, pp. 32–35; http://www.nato.int/docu/review/1998/9803-09.htm.

Brenner, Michael, ed., *NATO and Collective Security*, country chapters, New York: St. Martin's Press, Inc., 1998.

Brossard, Simon, "Altered Alliance," *Flight International*, April 28–May 4, 1999, pp. 32–34.

Brzeski, Andrzej, and Enrico Colombatto, "Can Eastern Europe Catch Up?" *Post-Communist Economies*, 11:1, March 1999, pp. 5–26.

Charter on a Distinctive Partnership Between the North Atlantic Treaty Organization and Ukraine, July 9, 1997; http://www.nato.int/docu.basictxt/ukrchrt.htm.

CIA, *The World Factbook* 2000; http://www.odci.gov/cia/publications/factbook/index.html.

Cichock, Mark A., "Interdependence and Manipulation in the Russian-Baltic Relationship: 1993–97," *Journal of Baltic Studies,* 30:2, Summer 1999, pp. 89–116.

Clemmesen, Brigadier-General Michael H., "Integration of New Alliance Members: The Intellectual-Cultural Dimension," *Defense Analysis,* 15:3, 1999, pp. 261–272.

Cohen, William S. (Secretary of Defense), *Annual Report to the President and the Congress,* 2000; http://www.dtic.mil/execsec/adr2000/.

Congressional Budget Office, "Integrating New Allies into NATO," Paper, Washington, D.C., October 2000.

Danreuther, Roland, "Escaping the Enlargement Trap in NATO-Russian Relations," *Survival,* 41:4, Winter 1999–2000, pp. 145–164.

Davis, Paul K., and Zalmay M. Khalilzad, *A Composite Approach to Air Force Planning,* RAND, MR-787-AF, 1996, pp. 17–19.

Director of Central Intelligence, "*Annual Report for the United States Intelligence Community (1999),*" May 2000; http://www.odci.gov/cia/publications/fy99intellrpt/dci_annual_report99.html.

Donnelly, Christopher, "Defense Transformation in the New Democracies," *NATO Review,* 44:6, November 1996, pp. 20–23; http://www.nato.int/docu/review/articles/9606–5.htm.

Doyle, Andrew, "Pole Position," *Flight International,* April 28–May 4, 1999, pp. 42–44.

Dunlop, John B., "Sifting Through the Rubble of the Yeltsin Years," *Problems of Post-Communism,* 47:1, January–February 2000, pp. 3–15.

Eckstein, Harry, Frederic J. Fleron, Jr., Erik P. Hoffmann, and William M. Reisinger, with Richard Ahl, Russell Bova, and Philip G. Roeder, *Can Democracy Take Root in Post-Soviet Russia? Explorations in State-Society Relations,* Lanham, MD: Rowman and Littlefield Publishers, 1998.

European Union, European Commission Reports on Progress Towards Accession; http://europa.eu.int/comm/enlargement/index.htm.

European Union, Reports on EU External Relations; http://europa.eu.int/comm/external_relations/see/intro/index.htm.

Fearon, James D., "Domestic Political Audiences and the Escalation of International Disputes," *American Political Science Review,* 88:3, September 1994, pp. 577–592.

Fish, M. Steven, *Democracy from Scratch: Opposition and Regime in the New Russian Revolution,* Princeton, NJ: Princeton University Press, 1995.

Forsberg, Tuomas, ed., *Contested Territory: Border Disputes at the Edge of the Former Soviet Empire,* Aldershot: Edward Elgar, 1995.

Founding Act on Mutual Relations, Cooperation and Security Between NATO and the Russian Federation, May 27, 1997; http://www.nato.int/docu/basictxt/fndact-a.htm.

Gaubatz, Kurt Taylor, "Democratic States and Commitment in International Relations," *International Organization,* 50:1, Winter 1996, pp. 109–139.

Gibson, James L., "Putting Up with Fellow Russians: An Analysis of Political Tolerance in the Fledgling Russian Democracy," *Political Research Quarterly,* 51:1, March 1998, pp. 37–68.

Glantz, David M., "Military Training and Education Challenges in Poland, the Czech Republic, and Hungary," *The Journal of Slavic Military Studies,* 11:3, September 1998, pp. 1–55 (part 1); "The Accomplishments, Strengths and Weaknesses of the U.S. Military (Security) Assistance Program," *The Journal of Slavic Military Studies,* 11:4, December 1998, pp. 1–71 (part 2); "Military Training and Educational Challenges in Poland, the Czech

Republic and Hungary; Conclusions and Recommendations," *The Journal of Slavic Military Studies*, 12:1, March 1999, pp. 1–12 (part 3).

Goldgeier, James M., *Not Whether But When; The U.S. Decision to Enlarge NATO,* Washington, D.C.: Brookings Institution Press, 1999.

Graham, Thomas E., "The Prospect of Russian Disintegration Is Low," *European Security*, 8:2, Summer 1999, pp. 1–14.

Hagelin, Bjorn, "Saab, British Aerospace and the JAS 39 Gripen Aircraft Joint Venture," *European Security*, 7:4, Winter 1998, pp. 91–117.

Hanson, Stephen E., and Jeffrey S. Kopstein, "The Weimar/Russia Comparison," *Post-Soviet Affairs*, 13:3, July 1997, pp. 252–283.

Henderson, Karen, "The Challenges of EU Eastward Enlargement," *International Politics*, 37:1, March 2000, pp. 1–17.

Herd, Graeme P., "Russia: Systemic Transformation or Federal Collapse?" *Journal of Peace Research*, 36:3, May 1999, pp. 259–269.

Herolf, Gunilla, "The Role of Non-Aligned States in European Defense Organizations: Finland and Sweden," in Mathias Jopp and Hanna Ojanen, eds., *European Security Integration: Implications for Non-Alignment and Alliances,* Programme on the Northern Dimension of the CFSP, Vol. 3, Institute for Security Studies, Western European Union, 1999.

Herspring, Dale R., *Requiem for an Army: The Demise of the East German Military*, Lanham, Maryland: Rowman and Littlefield, 1998.

Herspring, Dale R., "From the NVA to the Bundeswehr: Bringing the East Germans into NATO," in Andrew A. Michta, ed., *America's New Allies: Poland, Hungary, and the Czech Republic in NATO,* Seattle and London: University of Washington Press, 1999, pp. 12–39.

Huber, Reiner K., and Gernot Friedrich, *A Zero-Cost Option for NATO Enlargement: Arguments for a Comprehensive Approach*, The Potomac Papers, McLean, Virginia, August 1997.

Kaiser, Robert J. "Prospects for the Disintegration of the Russian Federation," *Post-Soviet Geography*, 36:7, September 1995, pp. 426–435.

Kamp, Karl-Heinz, "NATO Entrapped: Debating the Next Enlargement Round," *Survival*, 40:3, Autumn 1998, pp. 170–186.

Kemp, Ian, "NATO Advances Expansion Aims: Czech, Hungarian and Polish Integration Gathers Momentum," *International Defense Review*, April 2000, pp. 34–40.

Killingsworth, Paul S., Lionel Galway, Eiichi Kamiya, Brian Nichiporuk, Timothy L. Ramey, Robert S. Tripp, and James C. Wendt, *Flexbasing: Achieving Global Presence for Expeditionary Aerospace Forces*, RAND, MR-1113-AF, 2000.

Knight, Amy, *The Security Services and the Decline of Democracy in Russia: 1996–1999*, The Donald W. Treadgold Papers in Russian, East European, and Central Asian Studies, No. 23, October 1999, The Henry M. Jackson School of International Studies, The University of Washington, Seattle.

Kostadinova, Tatiana, "East European Public Support for NATO Membership: Fears and Aspirations," *Journal of Peace Research*, 37:2, 2000, pp. 235–249.

Kubicek, Paul, "Another Balkan Humpty-Dumpty: Putting Albania Back Together," *European Security*, 7:2, Summer 1998, pp. 78–91.

Kubicek, Paul, "Russian Foreign Policy and the West," *Political Science Quarterly*, 114:4, 1999–2000, pp. 547–568.

Laitin, David D., *Identity in Formation: The Russian-Speaking Populations in the Near Abroad*, Ithaca, NY: Cornell University Press, 1998.

Lake, David A., "Ulysses's Triumph: American Power and the New World Order, *Security Studies*, 8:4, Summer 1999, pp. 44–78.

Leeds, Brett Ashley, "Domestic Political Institutions, Credible Commitments, and International Cooperation, *American Journal of Political Science*, 43:4, October 1999, pp. 979–1002.

Lepgold, Joseph, "NATO's Post–Cold War Collective Action Problem," *International Security*, 23:1, Summer 1998, pp. 78–106.

Lesser, Ian O., *NATO Looks South: New Challenges and New Strategies in the Mediterranean*, RAND, MR-1126-AF, 2000.

Linden, Ronald H., "Putting on Their Sunday Best: Romania, Hungary, and the Puzzle of Peace," *International Studies Quarterly*, 44:1, 2000, pp. 121–145.

McFaul, Michael, "Russia's 'Privatized' State as an Impediment to Democratic Consolidation," *Security Dialogue*, 29:2, June 1998, pp. 191–199 (part 1), 29:3, September 1998 (part 2), pp. 315–332.

Mastny, Vojtech, "Reassuring NATO: Eastern Europe, Russia, and the Western Alliance," *Forsvarsstudier* (Defense Studies), Norwegian Institute for Defense Studies, No. 5, 1997.

Michta, Andrew A., "Poland: A Linchpin of Regional Security," in Andrew A. Michta, ed., *America's New Allies: Poland, Hungary, and the Czech Republic in NATO*, Seattle and London: University of Washington Press, 1999, pp. 40–73.

Mihalka, Michael, "Enlargement Deferred: More Political Instability for Romania? A Rejoinder," *Security Dialogue*, 30:4, December 1999, pp. 497–502.

The Military Balance, 2000–01. London: International Institute for Strategic Studies.

A National Security Strategy for a New Century, The White House, December 1999; http://www.pub.whitehouse.gov/uri-res/I2R?urn:pdi://oma.eop.gov.us/2000/1/7/1.text.1.

NATO, 1991 NATO Strategic Concept; http://www.nato.int./docu/basics.htm.

NATO, *The Alliance's Strategic Concept*, April 24, 1999; http://www.nato.int/docu/pr/1999/p99-065e.htm.

NATO, *Study on NATO Enlargement*, September 1995, paragraphs 4–7, 30, and 70–78; http://www.nato.int/docu/basictxt/enl-9501.htm.

NATO, Washington Summit Communique issued by Heads of State and Government participating in the meeting of the North Atlantic Council, Washington, D.C., April 24, 1999, point 7; http://www.nato.int/docu/pr/1999/p99–064e.htm.

NATO Parliamentary Assembly, Political Committee, Sub-Committee on NATO Enlargement and the New Democracies, *NATO-Russia Relations and Next Steps for NATO Enlargement*, Peter Viggers (rapporteur), September 28, 1999, paragraph 42.

Nelson, Daniel N., and Thomas S. Szayna, "NATO's Metamorphosis and Its New Members," *Problems of Post-Communism*, 45:4, July/August 1998, pp. 32–43.

Neuhold, Hanspeter, "The Austrian Debate on NATO Membership," in Anton A. Bebler, ed., *The Challenge of NATO Enlargement*, Westport, CT, and London: Praeger, 1999, pp. 188–194.

Ochmanek, David A., *NATO's Future: Implications for U.S. Military Capabilities and Posture*, RAND, MR-1162-AF, 2000.

O'Loughlin, John, Vladimir Kolossov, and Andrei Tchepalyga, "National Construction, Territorial Separatism, and Post-Soviet Geopolitics in the Transdniester Moldovan Republic," *Post-Soviet Geography and Economics*, 39:6, June 1998, pp. 332–358.

Orlova, Nina, and Per Ronnas, "The Crippling Cost of an Incomplete Transformation: The Case of Moldova," *Post-Communist Economies*, 11:3, September 1999, pp. 373–398.

Partell, Peter J., and Glenn Palmer, "Audience Costs and Interstate Crises: An Empirical Assessment of Fearon's Model of Dispute Outcomes," *International Studies Quarterly*, 43:2, June 1999, pp. 389–405.

Patterson, Christina M., David R. Markov, and Karen J. Richter, *Western-Style Armaments for New NATO Countries*, Institute for Defense Analyses, P–3450, June 1999.

Polsky, Yury, "Russian Nationalists' Worldview," *The Soviet and Post-Soviet Review*, 23:1, 1998, pp. 107–119.

Posen, Barry R., "The War for Kosovo: Serbia's Political-Military Strategy," *International Security*, 24:4, Spring 2000, pp. 39–84.

Pridham, Geoffrey, "Complying with the European Union's Democratic Conditionality: Transnational Party Linkages and Regime Change in Slovakia, 1993–1998, *Europe-Asia Studies*, 51:7, 1999, pp. 1221–1244.

Reed, William, "Alliance Duration and Democracy: An Extension and Cross-Validation of 'Democratic States and Commitment in International Relations,'" *American Journal of Political Science*, 41:3, July 1997, pp. 1072–1078.

Salminen, Esko, *The Silenced Media: The Propaganda War Between Russia and the West in Northern Europe*, New York: St. Martin's Press, 1999.

Sandler, Todd, "The Future Challenges of NATO: An Economic Viewpoint," *Defence and Peace Economics*, 8:4, 1997, pp. 319–353.

Sandler, Todd, "Alliance Formation, Alliance Expansion, and the Core," *Journal of Conflict Resolution*, 43:6, December 1999, pp. 727–747.

Sarvas, Stefan, "Professional Soldiers and Politics: A Case of Central and Eastern Europe," *Armed Forces and Society*, 26:1, Fall 1999, pp. 99–118.

Schimmelfennig, Frank, "NATO Enlargement: A Constructivist Explanation," *Security Studies*, 8:2–3, Winter 1998/99–Spring 1999, pp. 198–234.

Schmidt, Fabian, "Enemies Far and Near: Macedonia's Fragile Stability," *Problems of Post-Communism*, 45:4, July–August 1998, pp. 22–31.

Schoenbohm, Joerg, *Two Armies and One Fatherland: The End of the Nationale Volksarmee*, Providence and Oxford: Berghahn Books, 1996.

Sergounin, Alexander A., "Russian Domestic Debate on NATO Enlargement: From Phobia to Damage Limitation," *European Security*, 6:4, Winter 1997, pp. 55–71.

Shenfield, Stephen D., *Russian Fascism: Traditions, Tendencies, Movements*, New York: M. E. Sharpe, 2000.

Shlapentokh, Vladimir, "'Old,' 'New' and 'Post' Liberal Attitudes Toward the West: From Love to Hate," *Communist and Post-Communist Studies*, 31:3, September 1998, pp. 199–216.

Shlapentokh, Vladimir, "The Balkan War, the Rise of Anti-Americanism and the Future of Democracy in Russia," *International Journal of Public Opinion Research*, 11:3, Fall 1999, pp. 275–288.

Simon, Jeffrey, "Partnership for Peace (PfP): After the Washington Summit and Kosovo," *Strategic Forum*, No. 167, August 1999.

Skalnes, Lars S., "From the Outside In, from the Inside Out: NATO Expansion and International Relations Theory," *Security Studies*, 7:4, Summer 1998, pp. 44–87.

Smith, Alastair, "International Crises and Domestic Politics," *American Political Science Review*, 92:3, September 1998, pp. 623–638.

Smith, Michael, *Understanding Europe's New Common Foreign and Security Policy*, Institute on Global Conflict and Cooperation, Policy Paper No. 52, March 2000.

Sokolsky, Richard, and Tanya Charlick-Paley, *NATO and Caspian Security: A Mission Too Far?* RAND, MR-1074-AF, 1999.

Solomon, Gerald B., *The NATO Enlargement Debate, 1990–97: Blessings of Liberty*, Westport, CT, and London: Praeger, 1998.

Sweetman, Bill, "A Rising Imperative: More Demands for Airlift," *International Defense Review*, No. 2, 1998, pp. 22–31.

Szayna, Thomas S., "The Czech Republic: A Small Contributor or a 'Free Rider'?" in Andrew A. Michta, ed., *America's New Allies: Poland, Hungary, and the Czech Republic in NATO*, Seattle and London: University of Washington Press, 1999, pp. 112–148.

Thompson, Wayne C., "Citizenship and Borders: Legacies of Soviet Empire in Estonia," *Journal of Baltic Studies*, 29:2, Summer 1998, pp. 109–134.

Tismaneanu, Vladimir, *Nationalism, Populism, and Other Threats to Liberal Democracy in Post-Communist Europe*, The Donald W. Treadgold Papers in Russian, East European, and Central Asian Studies, No. 20, January 1999, The Henry M. Jackson School of International Studies, The University of Washington, Seattle.

Tkach, Vlada, "Moldova and Transdniestria: Painful Past, Deadlocked Present, Uncertain Future," *European Security*, 8:2, Summer 1999, pp. 130–159.

Tolz, Vera, "Conflicting 'Homeland Myths' and Nation-State Building in Postcommunist Russia," *Slavic Review*, 57:2, Summer 1998, pp. 267–294.

U.S. EUCOM, *Strategy of Readiness and Engagement*, 1998; http://www.eucom.mil/strategy/98strategy.pdf.

Wallensteen, Peter, and Margareta Sollenberg, "Armed Conflict, 1989–99," *Journal of Peace Research*, 37:5, 2000, pp. 635–649.

Waszczykowski, Witold, comments made at a round-table discussion at the Euro-Atlantic Association, Warsaw, April 9, 1999, as transcribed in "NATO-Nowe Wyzwania" (NATO-New Challenges), *Polska w Europie*, No. 29, August 1999, pp. 59–86.

The White House, *A National Security Strategy of Engagement and Enlargement*, Washington, D.C., GPO, July 1994.

Wohlforth, William C., "The Stability of a Unipolar World," *International Security*, 24:1, Summer 1999, pp. 5–41.

World Bank, World Bank Development Data; http://www.worldbank.org/data/countrydata/countrydata.html.

Wright, Joanne, "Trusting Flexible Friends: The Dangers of Flexibility in NATO and the West European Union/European Union," *Contemporary Security Policy*," 20:1, April 1999, pp. 111–129.

Yost, David S., "The New NATO and Collective Security," *Survival*, 40:2, Summer 1998, pp. 135–160.

Zakheim, Dov S., "Rationalizing and Coordinating the Sale of Conventional Armaments in Central and Eastern Europe," *International Politics*, 34, September 1997, pp. 303–326.